METROPOLITAN SAN DIEGO

METROPOLITAN PORTRAITS

Metropolitan Portraits explores the contemporary metropolis in its

diverse blend of past and present. Each volume describes a North

American urban region in terms of historic experience, spatial con-

figuration, culture, and contemporary issues. Books in the series

are intended to promote discussion and understanding of metro-

politan North America at the start of the twenty-first century.

JUDITH A. MARTIN, SERIES EDITOR

METROPOLITAN

SAN DIEGO

How Geography and Lifestyle Shape a New Urban Environment

LARRY R. FORD

University of Pennsylvania Press | Philadelphia

10 9 8 7 6 5 4 3 2 1

Published by

University of Pennsylvania Press

Philadelphia, Pennsylvania 19104-4011

Library of Congress Cataloging-in-Publication Data

Ford, Larry.

Metropolitan San Diego : how geography and lifestyle shape a new urban
environment / Larry R. Ford.

     p.   cm.—(Metropolitan portraits)

     ISBN 0-8122-3838-9 (cloth : alk. paper) — ISBN 0-8122-1898-1 (pbk. : alk. paper)

     Includes bibliographical references and index.

     1. Lifestyles—California—San Diego Metropolitan Area.   2. San Diego
Metropolitan Area (Calif.)—Social conditions.   3. San Diego Metropolitan Area
(Calif.)—Economic conditions.   I. Title.   II. Series

HQ2044 U62 S253—2004

307.76′09794′98—dc22   2004053570

CONTENTS

FOREWORD

Judith A. Martin

The Metropolitan Portraits Series seeks to understand and describe contemporary metropolitan regions in a fresh manner—one
that is informed and informative. Larry Ford was among the brave
few who first answered the challenge to describe his metropolitan
base this way. In some fashion, this is the book I had in mind
when I first began to think about this series. Along with other
colleagues around the country, Larry has an impressive familiarity
with his home region, honed by decades of teaching, engage-
ment, and observation. I could always get a great city tour from
Larry when visiting San Diego—now many others can share the
knowledge and insights formerly available only to students and
colleagues.

This is a book with several agendas, wrapped in a "good
read." On the one hand, it is a straightforward contemporary description of the people and places in the physical San Diego region. On the other hand, it is a story of the imagery conflict
embedded in a region that has almost perfect weather, great sce-
nery, a major military presence, and millions of new immigrants
in the past thirty to forty years. If there were a third hand, it would
hold the rather subversive critique of standard urban explanatory
variables that Ford launches here. Yes, San Diego is about capital
and class and race, as are other cities. But, as Ford persuasively

argues, in San Diego it is first about the ocean and the mountains, and what sorts of leisure options residents desire most.

From the first pages, describing his amazement at seeing students in shorts and students in parkas in his initial San Diego State class, Ford is closely tuned to the nuances and ironies of constructed identities all over the San Diego region. One such is the striking contrast between "Spanish" architecture neighborhoods and regular Latino neighborhoods, which typically lack such design signals. The image and reality tension that Ford ably poses forms the heart of his book. Here Ford's image critique extends that of his recent downtown book, suffusing his description of the San Diego region's emerging and evolving images over time, and demonstrating how these images have shaped regional growth patterns far out into La Mesa, Eastlake, and, yes, even Tijuana. A personal favorite is the way that San Diego willed a downtown into being in recent decades, making it a player in the national convention world. Tourists converge on the harbor, the Gaslamp Quarter, Horton Plaza, and Sea World, and perhaps ride the trolley to Tijuana. They seldom see the quite dense neighborhoods of the city—at all income levels—or the amazing topography that slices the city and region into sectors.

As with Carl Abbott's *Greater Portland* volume in this series, Ford's book examines the effects of the "old" West and the "new" West, as felt in San Diego. Interesting comparative possibilities begin to emerge. I do not know where this might lead, but I am grateful for the implied dialogue. *Metropolitan San Diego* offers a fresh perspective to local residents and to visitors who seek to understand more than the beach. I am delighted that *Metropolitan San Diego* has emerged.

CHAPTER ONE

San Diego Images: Inventing a Mediterranean Paradise

When I first arrived in San Diego over thirty years ago, I was amazed by its diversity. But it was a different kind of diversity from what one usually associates with big cities like New York or Chicago. For example, San Diego State University, my employer, is located midway between the beach communities to the west and the foothill settlements to the east. As I walked across campus during my first few weeks, I couldn't help noticing that some people were wearing tank tops and sandals while others were dressed in wool sweaters and down vests. How could this be? Could some people not read the weather report? The reality was that some students were coming from the cool and foggy coast where temperatures hovered around 60 degrees Fahrenheit while others were driving in from the near desert environment to the east where temperatures could approach 100.

The students differed in other ways as well. Those from the beach were likely to display the look of "surfers," with "bushy, bushy blond haircuts, Juarachi sandals too" (Beach Boys, 1963). Those from the foothills were likely to look "Western," with cowboy boots, checkered shirts, and blue jeans. They were sometimes referred to as "hodads" and tended toward the music of Merle Haggard. None of these differences were based on race, ethnicity, social class, or family heritage. Rather, they were examples of the "invented" cultures that emerged over the years in Southern California. This was not the kind of thing I found in the urban literature. Here were examples of looks and lifestyles that had evolved to fit the images and realities of particular types of physical environments. This was identity based on physical geography, reminiscent of the mountain tribes against the warriors from the plains, complete with conflicts over territory.

Over the decades, social diversity has become much more complicated and, to some degree, more "normal" with the arrival of vast numbers of people from around the United States and around the world. There are now, for example, Cambodian, Somali, Salvadoran, Russian, and Mexican neighborhoods, and the variations in wealth and status are more extreme. San Diego has become a big city with all the ethnic and social trappings implicit in this status. Still, the culture of place remains important. People still strongly identify with lifestyle zones that are largely based on the look of the land. Very few traditional generalizations or models of city structure are particularly helpful for San Diego. Metropolitan San Diego includes mountain cabins, tribal reservations, vast military bases, desert mobile home parks, urban barrios, beach resorts, downtown lofts, and border towns. It also includes, functionally if not officially, the city of Tijuana, Mexico.

The example of surfers verses hodads illustrates how the entire San Diego region has been influenced by outsiders who have come en masse seeking to find an exotic sense of place. Often they identify with distinctive types of physical settings and mythical pasts from beach towns and golf resorts to Spanish haciendas. Consequently, this analysis of the San Diego region revolves around considerations of cultural adaptations to this wildly varying physical environment. The bulk of the book, however, describes how these processes play out at the neighborhood level, including the many types of colorful local scenes that give the region its sense of place and identity.

All major American cities have a distinctive sense of place but San Diego is more unusual than most urban regions of its size. This book will explore not only many of the diverse places that make up the San Diego Metropolitan Area but also the processes of place creation that have shaped these communities along with the region as a whole. By so doing, I hope to shed light on the ways these processes are shaping every American urban region and neighborhood, albeit in (usually) more subtle ways.

INVENTING SAN DIEGO

The San Diego region has changed from a backwater with no discernable attributes to a paradise known throughout the country, if not the world, as a near-perfect place to live. This is a story of a harbor that the first European visitors ignored for over two centuries but that is now considered to be one of the great urban amenities of North America. It is, therefore, a story of not only the physical transformation of a place but also the changing image of a landscape in the context of changing societal values. It is very much in vogue these days to analyze the "invention" of culture, traditions, and places. This approach is particularly apt for San Diego. The city and its region have undergone numerous periods of boom and bust, and images have played an important role in these cycles. Such imagery is not unique to San Diego except in its extreme degree. Exploring the case of the San Diego region may shed light on the roles that perception and invented places have played throughout the American urban system.

Creating an image for San Diego has invoked seven themes, although a number of others could be discussed. The themes are all based on both myth and reality. They are (1) a long and exotic Spanish and Mexican past; (2) a Mediterranean landscape of flowers and gardens; (3) beach and bay lifestyles complete with surfing and sailing; (4) the military, especially a Navy town ambience; (5) the Mexican border; (6) the region as a center of innovation and technology; and (7) exotic and productive agriculture. Some of these overlap with southern California as a whole, but together they serve to build a distinctive San Diego personality. I begin with San Diego's long and partly imaginary colorful history.

NATIVE AMERICANS AND EARLY EXPLORERS

The San Diego area was occupied for several thousand years by a variety of Native American groups. Among them were the Kumeyaay, Luisenos, Cupenos, and Cahuillas. Today, there are eighteen reservations in the eastern foothills of the county, the first of them established in 1875. The native peoples did not practice agriculture and had no horses or other grazing animals. They relied on hunting (deer, rabbit, and quail) and gathering (especially acorns) along with fishing (lobsters, clams, octopus, and crabs) in the coastal lagoons. It is usual to say that they had little or no impact on the environment, but it is hard to say what many centuries of even slight human modifications might have been. Human-set fires, for example, could have changed the native vegetation in some areas. Still, compared to the woodlands of eastern North America and especially the central plateau of Mexico, the region was lightly occupied. It remained lightly occupied for a long time after the first Europeans "discovered" it as well.

Europeans first visited the region only fifty years after the initial voyage of Columbus. In 1542, the Spanish explorer Juan Cabrillo sailed into San Diego Bay while looking for a short-cut to China. Apparently his reports of the area were not glowing, since no other Europeans stopped by for another sixty years— Sebastian Vizcaino sailed in and named the bay San Diego de

Alcala, having arrived on the feast day of that name. In spite of the protected harbor, the somewhat desolate and lightly inhabited region did not appear promising; no other Europeans visited for another century and a half until Father Junipero Serra traveled overland from Mexico City in 1769 and established the first mission settlement. Even then, the goal was not really to fully occupy San Diego, but to establish a string of presidios (forts) and missions all along the coast of what was to become California. San Diego was first since it was the farthest south. It was neither the largest nor the most prosperous of the missions. It took a long time for anyone to think of San Diego as a paradise.

San Diego's low repute was a function of both its site and its situation. The physical attractions of the place seemed few at the time. It was semi-arid with few dependable water supplies, there were no accessible forests near the coast that could be used for house- or shipbuilding, and there was no evidence of mineral wealth in the form of gold or silver. Much of the bay was shallow, and muddy and brown chaparral covered the dusty hillsides nearby. It took some time even to find a suitable location for the mission, and it was moved inland to a preexisting Kumeyaay village with a better water supply in 1774. Despite a revolt by the native population against this takeover, permanent buildings were completed in 1784, largely with Indian labor. Europeans were still very few in number. By the late 1790s, about 1,400 native Americans lived, worked, or traded at the mission. In 1798, a second mission, San Luis Rey, was established along the river of the same name in what is today the northern part of the San Diego region. Neither place was urban by any stretch of the imagination.

The city of San Diego celebrated its Bicentennial in 1969 but it was hardly a village, let alone a city, until a half-century after Serra's initial arrival in 1769. Indeed, the population probably declined precipitously (possibly from 40,000 to 5,000) during the early years of the nineteenth century as disease and conflict decimated the natives. There was no significant European immigration, and it is estimated that there were only about 250 "whites" in San Diego in 1850.[1]

The situation, or relative location, of San Diego was even worse than its site. In the eighteenth century it was a very long way from anywhere. To get to San Diego by ship from Europe or northeastern North America meant going by way of either Cape Horn or the Cape of Good Hope. Both routes required many months of difficult travel. For many decades, San Diego was simply not worth the effort and so nobody came. Travel overland from Central Mexico or the American colonies was very difficult as well. Only dedicated padres and a few adventurous fur trappers made the effort until well into the nineteenth century. Ironically, the easiest journey was probably to cross the Pacific from East Asia. The Russians belatedly claimed Alaska and were working down the northern California Coast, but gave up the territories in the face of American interest (and money) after the Gold Rush. It would be interesting to know what California would have been like if motivated settlers from China, Japan, or other parts of Asia had arrived in great numbers during the eighteenth century.

CREATING A MEDITERRANEAN LANDSCAPE

As it was, the landscapes around the missions gradually changed during the Spanish Period (1769–1821) as new crops and animals were introduced. Logically, the padres sought to reproduce the landscapes and economies they knew in Spain and north central Mexico—a landscape that we often describe as Mediterranean. The Spanish grew grapes (and made wine), olives, oranges and lemons, and a variety of vegetables, usually with the aid of small dams and irrigation canals, since the climate was semi-arid rather than Mediterranean. They also introduced cattle, sheep, and horses. Still, prosperity was illusive. It took twice as much grazing land to raise a cow in San Diego than it did up the coast in moister Santa Barbara. Rainfall was not only minimal but also extremely variable from year to year and season to season, so it was hard to count on a good crop when water could be totally absent or arrive in the form of a flood.

Cattle and sheep took over a great deal of space, and mission Indians often worked as vaqueros or cowboys on the missions. Horses, along with guns, gave the Spanish soldiers a tremendous military advantage, and native revolts were not effective for long. The missions and presidios themselves were Spanish in architecture and layout. The gradual introduction of European decorative plants and the adaptation of native plants to courtyard settings eventually gave us the California-Spanish look we associate with the region today. The mythical "personality" of the region was taking shape. The combination of dirt roads and horse (and mule) carts connected at least a few areas such as the outlying missions or *asistencias* by the early decades of the nineteenth century, but access to the uplands of the interior remained poor. The Spanish imprint was tiny indeed.[2]

All this was happening just as the United States of America was being created on the eastern coast of North America. Boston was already nearly two hundred years old, but Anglo-American colonists were only just beginning to reach Ohio. Nevertheless, the new country was becoming aggressive in its search for new lands, resources, and trading partners. In matters of seaborne trade and commerce, New England led the way. The first United States ship (the *Betsey*) stopped at San Diego for wood and water in 1800. Yankee traders were beginning to bring commerce to San Diego Bay by 1821, when Mexico gained its independence from Spain and colonial trading restrictions were reduced. Mexico put trade regulations in place as well, hoping to focus activity in Monterrey, but these were lightly enforced. In 1833, Mexico secularized the missions, following the pattern of monastic lands in Europe, and vast private land grants became more common. Ranchos and rodeos became part of San Diego's romantic heritage. The ranchos were more interested than the missions in trade and sought ways to interest the Yankee traders. Between 1800 and 1828, about half the thirty or so ships that stopped in San Diego Bay were American, and by the 1820s the hide and tallow trade with New England had become dominant. Made famous by descriptions in Richard Henry Dana's *Two Years Before the Mast*, California gradually crept into Anglo-American awareness.[3] The ships from New England were veritable floating department stores and brought a variety of consumer items to the region for the first time. Even though there was no city per se in the San Diego area, the harbor had several important advantages. According to Dana's 1835 report, "For landing and taking on board hides, San Diego is decidedly the best place in California. The harbor is small and landlocked; there is no surf; the vessels lie within cable's length of the beach, and the beach itself is smooth, hard sand, without rocks or stones."[4] Boston traders were a common sight by the 1840s. The first major building in San Diego was a U.S. Army warehouse built in 1850 out of wood and bricks shipped around Cape Horn from Portland, Maine. By the mid-1850s, prefabricated houses such as the still existing Davis House (1857) were being shipped from New England. Wood was a scarce commodity in San Diego.

The region seemed destined to have a city, but there was little consensus about where to put it. The main population center for a long time was the Mission San Diego de Alcala, well inland from the port, but with secularization in the 1830s it was gradually abandoned. The presidio was a little closer to the harbor, but it lacked a reliable water supply and good agricultural land. Nevertheless, it was near here that the first "city" began to grow, com-

Mission de Acala. Restored missions have played an important role in creating San Diego's Spanish landscape.

plete with a typical *plaza mayor* and substantial adobe buildings. The sleepy Mexican village gained momentum when the United States took over California in 1848, but it was the 1849 Gold Rush that focused attention on all of California. In 1850, the City of San Diego was officially established and incorporated the vast tract of land (74 square miles) that had been part of the mission. It was huge in area but still largely devoid of people, as was San Diego county, which was also established in 1850 and included all southeastern California from Death Valley to San Diego Bay. The 1850 census counted a total population of 2,300 although it is difficult to say how accurate this figure was given the vast and minimally connected territory involved. By comparison, New York had about 700,000 people while Cincinnati and New Orleans counted about 115,000. San Francisco, the only "city" in California, had 34,000 inhabitants.

As the American Period dawned, it was evident that the City of San Diego was not only small but in the wrong place. The "port," little more than an off-loading beach, was located in Point Loma near what is now a Navy fuel depot at La Playa. The presidio and Mexican village were still much too far from any section of the waterfront. And so in 1867, Alonzo Horton established a new town on San Diego Bay. The development was known as "Horton's Folly" because of its relatively extensive and optimistic layout of blocks and lots.[5] In 1872, a major fire in the older settlement spurred movement toward the new harborside city and the Mexican village came to be known as Old Town. Old Town languished, but the new town did not exactly prosper either. The entire county had only 8,618 people in the 1880 census.

The first boom period in San Diego occurred in the late 1880s, as developers and entrepreneurs sought to entice and cajole people from the eastern United States to move to the region. Since there was really no reason to come, despite a very small and brief gold rush to the mountain village of Julian, attraction was based on myth and salesmanship. Before there could be immigration, however, there had to be a way to get there. An overland mail route was established in 1857, but it was not feasible to transport very many people to San Diego by stagecoach. Sailing trips around the Horn required motivation that most potential San Diego residents lacked. Such travelers more often were headed to San Francisco. Even though commerce and mail delivery were aided by the establishment of scheduled (if occasional) coastwise steamship service during the 1850s, the only reasonable way to move San Diego up the urban hierarchy was a railroad connection.

Plans for a railroad connection to the east first surfaced in 1869 but went nowhere. Lack of progress was due to San Diego having both too little and too much to offer. Since San Francisco interests were dominated by the railroad companies, they were not motivated to build a line to another excellent sheltered harbor in California. They could fail with either too much or too little business. Partly because of this potential competition and partly because of the rugged topography east of San Diego, the first rail lines (Southern Pacific) into southern California followed the relatively easy route from Yuma through Indio and Beaumont to Los Angeles. By 1876, Los Angeles, with no natural harbor but lots of flat, irrigable agricultural land, was set to take off as California's second major city. The best San Diego could hope for was a branch line to the north that would eventually hook up with the national network. Construction began in 1881, and by 1883 connections were complete to San Bernardino. In 1885 the line was extended to the rail hub at Barstow and San Diego was finally accessible via the Santa Fe to potential visitors from the rest of the country. The first transcontinental passenger train arrived in San Diego in November 1885, but the struggle to end the region's remoteness was not over.

The line to San Bernardino was washed out for nine months during a flood in 1884, and after a similar experience in 1891 it was abandoned. Fortunately, an alternative coastal line was built to Los Angeles in 1888, but by that time San Diego was so far behind its rival to the north that its rail connection was little more than a branch line to nowhere. As late as 1887, more visitors came to San Diego by steamship than by rail. Discriminatory fares did not help either—for awhile it was cheaper to come across the U.S. to Los Angeles than to continue down to San Diego. San Diego had to do something to make people want to visit. It needed an image that could help differentiate it from the plethora of southern California boomtowns gaining fame during the 1880s.

The boom ended with a crash in the late 1880s and the situation worsened with the national panic of 1893. The little San Diego settlement actually lost population during the early 1890s and remained a somewhat sleepy city, especially compared to Los Angeles and San Francisco. Some have argued that this failure to develop was a blessing in disguise. Lacking heavy industry and extensive rail yards, San Diego had to depend on its atmosphere and amenities to attract attention. It was not for the developers' lack of trying, however. As late as 1917, the famous "smokestacks versus geraniums" election between Louis Wilde and George Marston was won by (smokestack) Wilde, but few smokestacks appeared. Those who wanted to rely on sunshine and flowers got their way.[6]

USING HISTORY AND LEGEND TO CREATE AN URBAN IDENTITY

Even though most physical evidence of the Indian, Spanish, Mexican, and New England periods was gone (and precious little had ever existed), San Diegans were eager to create an idea of paradise that was at least partly based on historic images. The attempts are well illustrated by the overwhelming interest in the images, realities, and legends associated with Helen Hunt Jackson's 1884 novel *Ramona*.[7] The impact of the publication of *Ramona* is filled with irony. Jackson, who had already written an exposé on the plight of American indigenous peoples, set out to write a fictional work about exploited natives that would gain more attention for her cause. She hoped to write a sort of *Uncle Tom's Cabin* about Mexican and Yankee mistreatment of the native peoples of California. In 1881, she visited all the missions of California as well as a number of ranchos. She returned in 1883 having been appointed commissioner of Indian affairs by President Chester Arthur.

She concentrated on Riverside and San Diego as she developed the fictional story of an orphan, the child of a white father and an Indian mother, who is kept ignorant of her parentage while being raised in a foster home. She falls in love with a poor Indian sheepherder, Alessandro, but her foster mother hates Indians and refuses to let her see him. She runs away to be married by a sympathetic padre and goes to live with Alessandro's people. Their child dies of medical negligence and Allessandro is murdered before her eyes, but as an Indian she cannot bear witness to what happened. Meanwhile, Yankee farmers take the best land and force the natives farther into poverty. The book was meant to be a fictional "tear-jerker" that would rouse reformers to action. After all, it was based largely on factual events and real exploitation in real places.

Ramona did indeed have a terrific impact on the perception of life in southern California, but it was the opposite of what the author had intended. Set roughly from the 1820s to the 1850s, the period when many of the structures in old town San Diego were built, its vivid descriptions of Spanish-Mexican California and its people tended to coat the place and era in a romantic haze with sprawling haciendas and flower-filled courtyards. Rancho life was seen as enchanting, relaxed, and civilized, and Yankee intrusions as harsh and commercial. Within a year, the book had sold 15,000 copies, and it has been reissued 300 times since then. Very quickly, an entire tourist industry grew up around the Ramona myth and legendary life in southern California. Other stories, such as Zorro, with its chivalrous dons and dark-eyed senoritas, soon came along to boost the effort.

Thousands of postcards depicting various homes of Ramona and especially Ramona's marriage place, in reality the Casa de Estudillo in Old Town San Diego, were printed and sold, and locals and visitors alike began to confuse myth and reality to ever greater degrees. Since most of the actual buildings and landscapes associated with the Spanish and Mexican periods had long since fallen into disrepair, restoration efforts gained momentum with the widespread acceptance of Ramona imagery.

During the 1890s, campaigns were initiated to restore all of California's missions, although San Diego's Mission de Alcala was not completely redone until the 1930s. In addition, the Casa de Estudillo and the Casa Bandini, two of the more important buildings in Old Town San Diego, were rebuilt with considerable romanticized embellishment during the early years of the twentieth century. Significantly, John D. Spreckels, heir to a Hawaii sugar fortune and builder of San Diego's streetcar system, helped sponsor the restorations. Having historic sites at the end of the line was a good way to increase ridership. No sooner were these landmarks finished than throngs arrived to tour and photograph the historic "Spanish" settings. The legends grew, and by the 1920s Mary Pickford (Ramona) and Douglas Fairbanks, Sr. (Zorro) helped to publicize to all of America how romantic southern California could be. Today, two places listed on the National Register of Historic Sites are related to the Ramona myth.[8] In one case, the application actually contained the name "Casa Estudillo/Ramona's Marriage Place." In 1969, in honor of the two-hundredth anniversary of San Diego's "discovery," Old Town State Historic Park was officially created and dozens of new, authentic historic structures were built to complement those that had been romantically "restored." It is currently one of the region's major tourist attractions.

While Old Town emphasizes its Spanish/Mexican heritage, not all of San Diego's legendary past fits this category. A few of the restored buildings are quintessentially Yankee in architecture and function. The turn-of-the-twentieth-century downtown business interests usually sought the most up-to-date "American" architectural styles in order to demonstrate that the city had arrived. In addition, one of the main attractions on San Diego Bay (since 1927) is the *Star of India*, an 1857 sailing ship representing the coming of New Englanders to the shores of California. To a very real degree, San Diego has always had mixed feelings about its hybrid past and some of the conflicts still exist in current urban design issues. For example, the plaza mayor in Old Town was a barren, dusty "plaza de armas" when it was the center of the Mexican settlement, but Anglo settlers gradually planted grass

Casa de Estudillo in Old Town gained fame as "Ramona's Marriage Place" from the nine-teenth-century novel *Ramona*.

and (eucalyptus) trees after it passed into American hands. After all, parks should be green. When Old Town became an officially recognized historic theme district, suggestions were made that the greenery be removed in the name of authenticity. This was met with howls of opposition because today's tourists do not con-sider dusty plazas charming amenities. For close observers, the adobe and cacti restorations often look strange next to the green central park.

Spanish identity dominated San Diego's search for recognition during the early years of the twentieth century, but it was often based on wishful thinking rather than anything close to reality. Many visitors described San Diego as a barren, desolate, brown place well into the century. Spanish identity was more a plan for the future than a present identity. For one thing, there was the matter of water. The quest for a Mediterranean look required the creation of reliable water supplies. Small dams and piped water had been around since 1873, but the first golden age of reservoirs was the period 1887 to 1897, when six major dams were constructed on San Diego County streams. For a while, the region could rely on local runoff for its water supply. Through the 1930s, San Diego's growth required the constant construction of new dams. Without water, the desired Spanish look was impossible to maintain.[9]

The second boom in the mania for a romantic Spanish past came with the Panama-California Exposition in Balboa Park in 1915–16. In 1868, only a year after New Town San Diego was platted, a two-square mile area just to the northeast was set aside as City Park, in keeping with what was going on in New York, Philadelphia, San Francisco, and other leading American cities. The park was not just an altruistic venture, it also tended to focus real estate speculation in the core area and keep the new city from becoming a bunch of scattered ranchos. Later, transportation lines could be built directly out of the core along the margins of the park, again enhancing real estate speculation. For a long time, however, the park remained dusty and undeveloped. Something was needed to jazz up the image of both the city and its giant park. The answer came in the form of an exposition.

BALBOA PARK, THE EXPOSITION, AND CITY STATUS

The Panama-California Exposition, celebrating the opening of the Panama Canal and the connection of the East Coast to the West Coast by sea, was a major turning point for San Diego. A true world's fair was being held at the same time in the much larger city of San Francisco, but San Diego's regional effort was significant given its size and economy. More important, it put the city on the map for the first time. The park itself was renamed Balboa Park after the first European known to have seen the Pacific from American shores. The buildings created for the exposition were extraordinarily picturesque and many, especially the California

Tower, have remained nationally recognized symbols of the city. The buildings were all exuberantly Spanish. The central promenade, called the Prado, was lined with Spanish baroque or Churriguresque architecture that was far more elaborate than anything actually built in California during the Spanish heyday. Palm trees, bougainvillea, and a variety of Mediterranean and/or subtropical vegetation were used to enhance the exotic landscape of the fair. The city's Victorian train station was torn down and replaced with a Spanish version, as "Spain was bustin' out all over" in San Diego.[10]

While Spanish architecture established the look of the exposition, exotic vegetation played an important role as well. No place was this more evident than in the narrow canyons of the park that houses the San Diego Zoo. The zoo grew out of a temporary display at the exposition and gained a permanent place in the park in 1922. It is often said that the vegetation in the zoo is worth more than the animals, but it is hard to say for sure. Still, it is certainly true that the lush and enclosing environment does provide an ideal setting for the cries and growls of the animals concealed nearby.

With the Exposition leading the way, residential and commercial architecture soon followed suit. Many of the best residential neighborhoods laid out at the ends of the new streetcar systems during the 1920s were filled with replicas of Mexican adobe bungalows and Spanish haciendas. White stucco, red tiled roofs, and streets lined with towering palm trees were the norm in areas such as Kensington, Mission Hills, Point Loma, and La Jolla Village. San Diego's first apartment buildings and its many bungalow courts were also typically Spanish in appearance. Commercial districts and movie palaces also emphasized the exotic. The new (1931) campus of San Diego State College was uniformly Spanish in appearance, with a towering campanile as its theme building. In 1935 another fair, the California Pacific International Exposi-

The California Tower, built in Balboa Park in 1915, helped create San Diego's Spanish ambience.

tion, added to the architectural pizazz of Balboa Park. By then, even several downtown high-rises had red tile, as did many military structures.

Ironically, as San Diego became more Spanish in appearance it became more Anglo in population. New residents tended to be from the Midwest and South and the region became more "American" in culture and language. By 1940, the population of San Diego County, once part of Mexico, was only about 4 percent Hispanic. But the new residents found the mythical Spanish heritage to be appealing. In the neighborhoods around San Diego as well, the more Spanish the architecture, the more Anglo the population. While Anglo-Americans flocked to the charming Spanish bungalows during the first half of the twentieth century, the increasingly marginalized Latino population were largely left to occupy the older Victorian and Craftsman cottages. This irony continued through the 1970s as minority populations often occupied postwar tract homes while wealthier people sought the charm of old San Diego. Today, with red tile and stucco covering most of the county, it is less easy to observe such obvious correlations.

Other Mediterranean themes supported the exotic claims of San Diego during the early 1900s. Real estate ads and tourist brochures sometimes described San Diego as "Our Italy" because of its climate, vegetation (and wine), and Mediterranean coastal village ambience. La Jolla and Point Loma were thought to be Amalfi-like. This image was supported by the arrival of Italian and Portuguese fishermen to the San Diego harbor, and the city soon became associated with its tuna fleet and very real seafood and Italian restaurants, as well as its mythical past.

LIFE ON THE BEACH

In 1885, a consortium led by Elisha Babcock and Hampton Story purchased a large peninsula in the middle of San Diego Bay for a total sum of $110,000. Their intent was to build a seaside resort community similar to those being built in the East. The hope was that such a place would appeal to visitors to the now railroad-accessible San Diego. In 1886, ferry service was established to the "island" of Coronado and lots were auctioned. With money in hand from the auction, work was begun on the massive Hotel del Coronado. It was completed in 1888 and soon became an important symbol for the sleepy city of San Diego. Money from millionaire John D. Spreckels helped to keep the operation going until its fame could be established. Thus began a second dimension of San Diego's image, "Surf City."

The hotel was located between the ocean beach and Glorietta Bay, an ideal spot for aquatic activities. It was accessible by a combination of ferry and streetcar from the rail terminal in downtown San Diego. At first the hotel was aimed only at a wealthy clientele of presidents, movie stars, and royalty. By 1900, however, a vast Tent City was established next door that brought thousands of families to Coronado for a summer beach vacation complete with carnival booths, a Ferris wheel, sailing, and a variety of swimming facilities. Tent City continued until 1939, and the "Del" itself still stands as the oldest wooden Victorian hotel in America. It has been used in several popular films such as *Some Like It Hot* and *The Stuntman*.[11]

With Coronado, a separate city after 1891, leading the way, several other beach towns were developed by the turn of the twentieth century. Chief among them were Ocean Beach, Pacific Beach, Del Mar, and La Jolla. By the early 1920s, Spreckels had built a streetcar line to a large amusement park complete with a roller coaster in the middle of the quintessential oceanfront community of Mission Beach. Over the years, a number of north county beach towns were developed between Oceanside and Del Mar. With the introduction and popularization of the sport of Hawaiian surfing during the 1920s, a California subculture was born.

The Hotel del Coronado, built in 1888, helped make San Diego an important destination as a beach resort.

Although San Diego was rarely depicted in surf movies (such as *Gidget* and *Beach Blanket Bingo*) the image of the beach as a focal point for life in the region has always loomed large in the minds of both residents and visitors. One of the reasons is that over 80 percent of the 70 miles of beaches in San Diego County are publicly owned and most, except for military bases, are open to all. This contrasts mightily with the situation in many eastern states where public access to beaches is difficult or expensive.

While water-related recreation in San Diego is obviously associated with the physical geography of the region, it is not always the natural environment that is the attraction. The region has modified its shoreline in significant ways. Beginning in the 1950s, a huge (4,900-acre) area of mudflats and marshes once known as False Bay was dredged and reshaped into a recreation and tourist zone called (you guessed it) *Mission* Bay. The result is a series of islands, peninsulas, beaches, harbors, marinas, and picnic areas just inland from Mission Beach. Over 90 percent of the area is a designated city park. Although some beaches have been closed

Beach and boats on Mission Bay perpetuate the image of San Diego as a beach town.

several times in recent years due to sewage spills and polluted run-off from city streets, Mission Bay Park is normally filled with people (and cars) all year.[12]

San Diego Bay has also been greatly modified over the past century. Over three square miles of fill land have been created as the bay was dredged for deeper ship channels. This new land is now occupied by the airport, several military installations, highways, marinas, and parks. Embankments that replaced the constantly shifting mudflats of earlier times have made the shoreline permanent. Two peninsulas (like Coronado, referred to as islands) were also constructed during the 1950s and 1960s in San Diego Bay using material dredged for ever larger Navy vessels. Harbor Island and Shelter Island occupy the approximate place where the San Diego River entered the Bay before it was rerouted and channeled (beginning in 1875) to flow directly to the ocean. They are artificial extensions that house both public parks and a variety of hotels and restaurants. Similar developments such as Marina Park were later created in downtown San Diego. All around San Diego Bay, fill land has been used to modify the shoreline.

Sandy beaches occupy most of the region's ocean shoreline, but even these are not entirely natural. With water in short supply, dams have been built on all the rivers that empty into the ocean, so sand is not adequately replenished by run-off. In addition, breakwaters and piers have interfered with the seasonal north and south movements of beach sand. As a result, some beaches have diminished in size and others have grown. Today, imported sand from dredging and other sources is sometimes used to make up the losses suffered through "natural" processes.[13] Still, "the beach" and related activities such as surfing, sailing, and water skiing play a very important role in the national image of San Diego. For example, the city got international attention when the America's Cup sailboat races were held off San Diego. Several television shows such as *Simon and Simon* were also filmed on San Diego beaches.

Because of its closeness to the center of the film and television industry in Los Angeles and its wide variety of physical and human landscapes, San Diego settings have often been used in feature films. Surprisingly, however, the region has an almost nonexistent film personality. While both Los Angles and San Francisco have many famous landmarks and neighborhoods that are used regularly in feature films, San Diego is most often used for a generic place rather than a specific locale. While Los Angeles has the City Hall, Hollywood Sign, Malibu, Beverly Hills, Venice, Wilshire Boulevard, and many other famous and recognizable places, the most commonly filmed setting in San Diego is a marina in Mission Bay that often substitutes for Florida, Hawaii, Texas, or even Los Angeles. It is anywhere, U.S.A. Similarly, San Diego's downtown is often used, but mainly for its generic alleys, warehouses, and historic buildings rather than anything notable. Western or country scenes are filmed in the nearby foothills and mountains, but again the place is rarely specified. It could be argued that despite its potential imageability, San Diego does not have a recognizable film image. Even the Hotel del Coronado, perhaps the region's most famous building, was supposed to be in Florida in the movie *Some Like It Hot*.

Perhaps one measure of a city's arrival as an important American place is that its landscape is so well known that it is immediately recognizable in movies and advertisements. New York, Chicago, San Francisco, Miami, New Orleans, and a few others are already there. The diverse San Diego landscape, however, still contributes mainly to a stealth image of vaguely San Diego-like generic settings. Establishing and selling an urban region's image and personality is a tricky business. Maintaining this image in the face of changing realities can be even trickier.

The physical geography of inland areas has also been used in the creation of a San Diego image, but to a much lesser degree. Rock climbing, dune buggy rides in the desert, and hikes in mountain parks are all very much a part of life in metropolitan San Diego but are not so well integrated into the personality of the region. I discuss additional aspects of San Diego's physical realm later in the book. Still, it is interesting to point out that in one (long) weekend it is possible to sail in the ocean, play volleyball at the beach, climb a 6,000-foot mountain, gamble at an Indian casino on one of many reservations, visit a winery and the Wild Animal Park, and hike through a desert, all without leaving the San Diego Metropolitan Area.

THE NAVY TOWN PERSONALITY

During the nineteenth century, many visitors to San Diego prophesied that it would become the major metropolis of southern California since it had a marvelous protected harbor that no other city, including Los Angeles, could match. Ironically, San Diego has never been a significant port. With the growth of Los Angeles and the completion of the artificial harbors at San Pedro and Long

Beach during the second decade of the twentieth century, it was easier to use trains and trucks from these to handle San Diego's meager trade. Thus, one of the West Coast's best harbors has always been relatively devoid of commercial activity.

Such was the situation when San Diego was designated a Navy base during the Spanish-American War of 1898. For a while, little activity resulted, but when Teddy Roosevelt's Great White Fleet visited San Diego Bay in 1908, some important people were impressed with the harbor, and the tide turned. With the opening of the Panama Canal and the acquisition of Pacific territories such as the Philippines and Hawaii, the United States became increasingly interested in a full-fledged, two-ocean Navy. Although naval facilities were gradually constructed all up and down the West Coast, San Diego became the largest and most famous. This was partly because the Navy was for a long time the biggest and most visible game in town. This was not true in Los Angeles or San Francisco.

World War I served to speed up the establishment of military facilities in San Diego, and by 1917 Camp Kearny and North Island (Coronado) Naval Air Station were operating. Military installations evolved gradually until the advent of World War II, when San Diego County became one of the nation's major centers of Navy and Marine activity. Camp Pendleton Marine Base, the largest base in the United States, opened in 1942 using the site of the old Rancho Santa Margarita land grant in the northern part of the county near Oceanside. By the time the war was over, about ten square miles of land on San Diego Bay was occupied by various military bases, and the bay itself was full of everything from aircraft carriers to destroyers. As late as the 1950s, it was estimated that two-thirds of the San Diego economy was directly or indirectly related to military spending.[14] Despite cutbacks in this spending, San Diego has actually benefited from base consolidation and remains a Navy town. Both active ships and a huge "moth ball" fleet occupy much of the shoreline of San Diego Bay. Military aircraft from North Island are a constant sight, although the noisiest helicopters have been moved to Miramar Naval Base in suburban San Diego.

The Navy has traditionally played an important role in the region's celebrations and holiday festivities. On the Fourth of July and other patriotic holidays, Navy skydivers, Seal teams, and gunships often demonstrate their training skills for large audiences. Military bands are expected at every local parade and uniformed Navy personnel often occupy special sections at sporting events.

In spite of its overwhelming presence, the Navy has in some ways diminished its impact on everyday life in the city. Until September 11, Navy ships often occupied a downtown pier and were open for tourist visits on a regular basis. These days, everyone, including those in sailboats, must keep at least 100 yards away from military vessels. On the other hand, the *Midway*, a retired aircraft carrier, is now berthed in downtown San Diego and is open for business as a Navy museum.

Downtown revitalization has also taken a toll on the Navy look of the town. From the 1940s through the 1970s, downtown San Diego, as well as the centers of other towns such as Oceanside and National City, was filled with establishments aimed at sailors. Especially visible were bars, strip joints, locker clubs, and tattoo parlors, but there were also game arcades and "hip" clothing stores. Today most of these places are gone. Gone, too, are massive numbers of sailors strolling the streets in uniform. San Diego is still a Navy town, but its profile is a bit lower these days.

THE MEXICAN BORDER

One aspect of the San Diego personality that cannot be contested by Los Angeles and other cities is that it is in on the Mexican bor-

The retired aircraft carrier *Midway* serves as a military museum on San Diego's downtown waterfront.

der. Although downtown San Diego is actually about fifteen miles from the border crossing at Tijuana, the area between is solidly built up, and many residents on both sides of the fence stare at homes and businesses in a different country. Today the San Diego-Tijuana border crossing is the busiest in the world—and that is only counting legal crossings. The greater San Diego-Tijuana region is also the largest bicultural, bilingual urban area in the world (except perhaps for Detroit-Windsor). This alone should make life in San Diego different from that in most U.S. cities.[15] Before exploring this issue, however, it is important to point out that the border, like the other topics discussed above, is at least partly romanticized.

The border of course only began its existence with the independence of California from Mexico in 1848, and for a long time there were so few people on either side that it did not matter much to anybody. The Treaty of Guadalupe Hidalgo set the boundary so as to have all of San Diego Bay within the United States. That settled, the border was little more than a line on the map.

The Mexico-United States border at Tijuana. Mexico is on the left.

Interest increased when issues of boundary waters arose in 1889. The presence of Mexican revolutionaries caused concern in 1911, when battles in Tijuana brought the U.S. Army to San Diego to guard the border. World War I also led to increased border restrictions.

The border of myth and legend, however, emerged with the advent of Prohibition in 1918, when eager entrepreneurs arrived to fill a need. Suddenly the border became a business opportunity. Tijuana (then called Zaragoza) was little more than a tiny cattle ranching settlement until the 1880s. It was a long way from central Mexico with practically nonexistent transportation and so was always tied to the California economy. When railroads and land booms arrived in California during the 1880s, some thought that similar opportunities might exist on the other side of the border.

A plan for the city of Tijuana was only created in 1889, and during the 1890s it was said to have more saloons than buildings. The city only had about 1,000 people in 1900, but activity increased when it was connected by rail to San Diego in 1906. By

1916, Tijuana had a racetrack and began to reach out to visitors from the north. This was the calm before the storm. The combination of Prohibition and new paved highways to San Diego and Los Angeles made Tijuana the quintessential border town during the 1920s. Americans came from far and wide to drink, dance, gamble, see bullfights, shop, and otherwise stretch convention. Tijuana's exotic landscape of colorful bars, strip clubs, casinos, jai lai palaces, racetracks, and boxing arenas helped to give the place a "sin city" reputation that has been difficult to overcome. As late as 1958, "Just send my mail to the Tijuana jail" was a hit refrain song in the U.S. The city's architecture and signage were described as resulting from what Mexicans think Americans think Mexico is.

For a long time, Tijuana was even more integrated into the San Diego economy than it is today, since many of the businesses and even many of the employees there were Americans. The city was a small California operation that simply took advantage of the existence of an international border to make profits. As Tijuana grew, it gradually became both more diverse and more Mexican. By 1940, the city had over 20,000 inhabitants as new roads from the Mexican interior made getting there easier. As Tijuana edged closer to being a real Mexican town, it became something of an embarrassment as well. In 1935, the Mexican government sought to clean up Tijuana's image by making gambling illegal and closing the major casinos. This action probably helped pave the way for the rise of Las Vegas a few years later. To make up for losses to its economy, the border region was declared a free trade zone and programs were put in place to foster industrialization.

Political leaders on the northern side of the border have often seen Tijuana as problematic as well. Several attempts were made over the decades to limit travel across the border, especially during wartime. During one period, the U.S. closed the border at 9 p.m. in order to limit debauchery, but this only served to create a hotel industry in Tijuana. Today, San Diego police keep a watchful eye out for underage drinkers heading back into San Diego after a night in "TJ" discos.

In recent decades, Tijuana, Ensenada, and indeed much of northern Baja California have become integrated into the San Diego region in different and more respectable ways. With about 1.5 million people, Tijuana provides both inexpensive labor and a steady supply of shoppers for San Diego businesses. Over the past three decades, maquiladoras (factories specializing in labor intensive operations) have sprung up all along the Mexican border, and Tijuana has been a leader in this trend. Materials can be imported from the U.S., processed or finished in Mexico, and sent back to the U.S. as final products. Tijuana has thus benefited from not only North American but also Japanese and European investment. The number of maquiladoras has probably peaked, and the impact of NAFTA remains to be seen. It may encourage trade with the Mexican interior at the expense of the border now that the latter's special status has been diminished. Still, Tijuana is a wealthy city by Mexican standards, and it is still growing rapidly. Buses from Mexico can be seen regularly at San Diego attractions and shopping centers.

For these reasons and more, San Diego is now and always has been a border town. Except for the arbitrary rules of the U.S. Census, Tijuana would probably be officially part of the San Diego Metropolitan Area. As it is, it is certainly a very important unofficial part. Interestingly, the existence of a nearby border probably keeps San Diego from becoming more Latino in culture. Since San Diego is so handy and accessible for the residents of Tijuana, there is little reason to live there. Housing and other costs are much lower south of the border, so San Diego lacks the kinds of immense barrios found in say Los Angeles or San Antonio. Currently, San Diego County is about 27 percent Latino, a figure including many long time residents as well as recent in-migrants.

A CENTER OF RESEARCH AND TECHNOLOGY

Compared to the industrial cities of the East, relatively few inventions and innovations occurred in San Diego during the early decades of the twentieth century. Still, the region has always considered itself to be on the cutting edge of at least some kinds of new technology and new ways of doing things. In no field has this been truer than flight. Aviation research not only led to some important breakthroughs in San Diego, but these were high-profile developments that gained the city inordinate fame early on. Chief among these was the building of the plane that Lindbergh used for his solo transatlantic flight in 1927 at San Diego's Ryan Aircraft. Although the plane was dubbed the Spirit of St. Louis because it was financed there, it actually began its trip to Paris by taking off from San Diego en route to its official start in New York. In 1928, San Diego's new airport was named Lindbergh Field.

A number of other flight-related events gave San Diego other firsts. The first seaplane test flights (1912), the first in-flight refueling (1923), and the home port for the first aircraft carriers (1930s) helped to give San Diego the title "Air Capital of the United States." When John Glenn became the first person to circle the globe (1961), he did so using an Atlas rocket made in San Diego. The aerospace industry evolved even before World War II broke out, with thousands of employees working at Consolidated Aircraft Corporation (later Convair). But it was the war that brought rapid growth to the region. San Diego firms were busy producing military and civilian aircraft, missiles, weapons, rockets, and other paraphernalia, and people poured in from all over the country to work at the plants. San Diego became a big city during the 1940s, with the metropolitan population passing the 500,000 mark in the 1950 census.

In spite of booms and busts with changing patterns of defense spending, San Diego has remained a center of aerospace innovation, though that role is less dominant now. As one pundit put it, the Cold War saved San Diego from the "ravages of peace."[16] Firms such as Convair (later absorbed by General Dynamics), Ryan, Rohr, and Solar produced multiple specialized components, making San Diego somewhat defense dependent through the 1970s.

Since then, however, innovations have become more diversified. The Scripps Institute of Oceanography pioneered underwater research, and biomedical research blossomed in association with the 1960 campus of the University of California. An important pharmaceutical industry has grown out of this relationship with leaders such as Isis and Idec. More recently, telecommunications and other aspects of the high-tech world have boomed with the advent of corporations like Qualcomm, Cubic, and Cox. Software boomed in the 1990s along with various types of electronic equipment. In addition, San Diego has also emerged as a leader in leisure products such as portable spas, golf equipment, and sailboats. Manufacturing is now the leading economic sector in the county, but it is not heavy industry. San Diego's industry is largely a matter of many small companies emphasizing research and development and the manufacture of small, specialized, easily transportable items.[17] San Diego is poorly located and equipped to be a distribution center since it lacks good rail and highway connections and, ironically, even a substantial airport. It must rely on attracting businesses that can pay high rents, occupy relatively small spaces, and feel that they benefit from the fact that a large number of scientists and other innovators like to live here. Everyone agrees that San Diego's economic health is based in part on its remaining an attractive place, but just what this means in terms of environmental policy is often difficult to work out.

Exotic agriculture and signage in Fallbrook, in San Diego's North County.

EXOTIC AND PRODUCTIVE AGRICULTURE

Agriculture has always played an important role in San Diego's image, from the early Spanish ranchos to the later introduction of exotic Mediterranean crops such as oranges and lemons. Many of the small towns surrounding the city were originally agricultural settlements, and some, like Lemon Grove, reflect those origins in their names. Primary production, including agriculture, mining, and fishing, is still an important part of the regional economy but the former is dominant.

Part of the reason for the importance of agriculture in the metropolitan region is the vast size of San Diego County. Unlike most metropolitan areas in the eastern United States, San Diego County, the official SMSA, includes 4,225 square miles—it is bigger than the states of Delaware and Rhode Island combined and almost as big as Connecticut. In addition, also unlike most American metropolitan areas, San Diego has not grown by adding new counties as they have become functionally integrated with the central city. San Diego County has always been huge and has always contained heavily agricultural districts (as well as national forests and deserts) within its boundaries. The rustic imagery, therefore, goes back to the beginning, and there are still many nooks and crannies that are ideal for certain crops. There is even a substantial amount of agriculture within the city limits of San Diego, since it is "overbounded" and contains about 324 square miles of land.

Today, agriculture ranks in the top four economic activities in the metropolitan area, generating about 3.1 billion dollars per year. While space-extensive pursuits such as ranching have moved to remote mountain valleys well away from suburban growth, high value crops are still quite visible in the urban region. The most famous are cut flowers and avocados, but citrus crops, tomatoes, eggs, and dairying are still important.[18]

The flower industry is booming, since fresh cut flowers can now be airfreighted to all corners of the world quickly and efficiently and the demand is high. Avocados thrive as well: San Diego County accounts for nearly the entire U.S. production. Both of these crops are labor intensive and high value. Citrus fruit, eggs, and vegetables are more vulnerable to urban sprawl, but the growing local market keeps demand high. The cost and availability of water as well as the cost of land may make agriculture more problematic in the future, but there are currently several officially designated agricultural preserves located throughout the county.

COMBINING MYTH AND REALITY

San Diego was still very small as the twentieth century began, but most of the components of its regional image either were already in place or soon would be. The entire county had perhaps 35,000 people in 1900, while the sprawling city of 74 square miles had fewer than 18,000. Other West Coast cities were far ahead in population and economic development. San Francisco, for example, housed about 340,000 people, and Portland, Oregon, had over 90,000. More important, Los Angeles had grown to over 100,000 leaving San Diego to be a permanent "little sister." San Diego was already gaining a reputation for its Spanish (Ramona) heritage, Mediterranean (including agricultural) landscapes, beach resorts, gateway to Mexico, and Navy ships, but it was piling up myths and legends a lot faster than it was building things of substance. As discussed above, the Spanish legend was pervasive long before the place really looked very Spanish. Despite phenomenal growth during the twentieth century, however, these images have remained remarkably persistent even in the face of an additional three million people. Many of the images are embedded in the area's place names. For example, a resident of a coastal community called Mission Beach, Ocean Beach, or Pacific Beach can take a road like Nimitz, Midway, or Rosecrans (military names) to Friars Road in Mission Valley to watch the Padres play baseball. San Diego has continued to try to build on its strengths, but there may be limits. With millions of cars, very little water, and a lack of affordable housing, changes may have to come.

SAN DIEGO IMAGINED

The diagram shown here is one way of illustrating the past and present image of the San Diego metropolitan region and its context. The core is made up of three roughly equal sectors—Aquatic, Mediterranean, and High-Tech. The Aquatic includes the Navy, tuna fishing, sailboats, ferries, surf boards, cargo vessels, water skiers, and tour ships. It is dominated by images of the coastal beaches, bays, marinas, and lagoons that occupy nearly all the metropolitan area's 60+ miles of coastline.

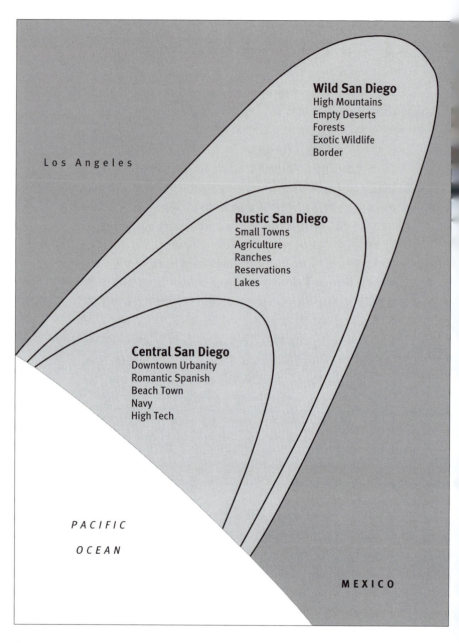

Wild San Diego
High Mountains
Empty Deserts
Forests
Exotic Wildlife
Border

Los Angeles

Rustic San Diego
Small Towns
Agriculture
Ranches
Reservations
Lakes

Central San Diego
Downtown Urbanity
Romantic Spanish
Beach Town
Navy
High Tech

PACIFIC

OCEAN

MEXICO

The concentric zones of San Diego County.

The central core is also made up of a picturesque Mediterranean city focusing on landmarks such as Balboa Park and the Interwar Spanish Colonial neighborhoods. To some degree, this image has been enhanced by the recent wave of enthusiasm for postmodern architecture and whimsical, colorful, places such as Horton Plaza Shopping Center and Seaport Village. The third component of the center is the modern, high-tech images of gleaming office parks, aerospace facilities, and biomedical labs.

To the east, the second ring focuses on agricultural land, ranches, and quaint mining towns such as Julian, with its "countrified" look and annual Apple Days festival. This region becomes increasing hilly inland toward the mountains and often exudes a studied rusticity of "wild west" architecture, country and western dance halls, and a generally libertarian attitude toward aesthetics. The third zone is the high mountain parks and Cleveland National Forest. This is hiking country where cougars can occasionally be seen. It even snows here, and many San Diegans flock to a usually short-lived winter scene. Finally, in the shadow of the Laguna Mountains lies the low desert with its unusual vegetation and creatures.

To the south lie the Mexican border and the love-hate relationship that accompanies it. A major tourist attraction and an important economic asset in many ways, it is also a source of (illegal) immigration and some degree of smuggling and crime. The real threat, however, is to the north. The five-county Greater Los Angeles area contains about fourteen million people as well as a pace of life that is very un-San Diegan. Perhaps Los Angeles, so often associated with abnormality in American literature, actually represents the coming to idyllic San Diego of normal America with its traffic, crime, industry, pollution, ghettos, and vast housing tracts. A typical San Diegan will often remark, "Thank God for Camp Pendleton and its eighteen miles of [empty] military land—it forms the only defense we have against Los Angeles."

Kevin Lynch's book *Image of the City* provides one more set of insights for understanding the San Diego region.[19] Lynch explored the mental maps that people carry in their heads for cities that they know well. He distilled these perceptions into five categories—nodes, landmarks, edges, paths, and districts—and displayed each of these in the form of sketch maps as well as verbal descriptions. He argued that good places are imageable or legible in that they can be read and understood relatively easily. People will explore an area that they understand and feel comfortable in more readily than a place that is confusing and frustrating. They will tend to avoid places that either have no image or jumbled ones. At the metropolitan level, San Diego turns out to be very imageable. It can be argued, therefore, that its desirability can be understood in these "imageability" terms as well as the usual factors such as climate and beaches.

Compared to many metropolitan areas roughly its size, such as Atlanta or Houston, San Diego has very precise edges. It is clearly bounded on all four sides. There is the Pacific Ocean to the west, the mountains to the east, Mexico to the south, and Camp Pendleton to the north. You are either in San Diego or you are not as there are clear gateways to the metropolitan region. In addition, the edges are generally "friendly"—they are not rail yards, toxic waste dumps, or swamps. They are enclosing but not confining. In the same way that conceptions of paradise are usually associated with bounded spaces such as an island or a valley, San Diego can be viewed as occupying a special, largely physical, niche that is clearly defined.

San Diego has a number of well-known and highly visible landmarks as well. These include famous peaks and hills (sometimes with controversial crosses on top), other major physical features such as Mission Valley and Mission Bay, and architectural ones such as the Coronado Bridge, the city skyline, and Seaworld Tower. In addition, the hilly and relatively treeless urban area

San Diego from the air. Canyons help establish and maintain the identities of separate neighborhoods.

makes long vistas the norm. It is easy to tell where you are in the urban area compared to flat cities with lots of trees or big buildings. You know what direction you are traveling and roughly how long it will take to get to your destination. This is what imageability means.

San Diego also gets high marks for its imageable districts. Neighborhoods are often defined by physical boundaries as well. Examples include island communities like Coronado, peninsula communities like Mission Beach, and hilltop communities like Mount Helix. Many neighborhoods are located on mesas separated by canyons from areas nearby. In addition, a large number of districts are associated with a particular microclimate or elevation and so there are "mountain" towns, beach towns, and valley towns. More traditional variations in neighborhood type such as those having to do with differences in wealth, ethnicity, and age have been layered in on top of the pronounced physical characteristics. There is no mistaking Pacific Beach and Fallbrook. These districts and the lifestyles associated with them will be the focus of much of this book.

The remaining two elements of imageability, paths and nodes, are less well developed in San Diego, but they are far from nonexistent. While there are few "great streets" of the caliber of the Champs Elysées or New York's Fifth Avenue, there are some pretty good paths with a lot of memorable character winding through the urban area. Many of the highways go through canyons or valleys and so they are green (or brown depending on the season) if nothing else. Others follow the shoreline or a ridge and offer far-off views. There are also an increasing number of good urban streets with an interesting architectural or ethnic flavor. Still, too many are bland, suburban roadways with the usual strip malls and garage doors and these are the kinds that are most rapidly increasing in number.

Finally, San Diego has some good nodes or multi-purpose

coming together places but not nearly enough for an urban area covering more than 4,000 square miles. Downtown is booming and its skyline of office buildings, hotels, and condominiums is visible from many miles away. With scores of restaurants, theaters, and waterfront promenades it has become a gathering place for tourists and locals alike. It is not really a very dominant downtown for business though, and it pales by comparison with those of San Francisco or Chicago. The Prado in Balboa Park and the region's many beach communities also serve as gathering places. Some suburban communities such as La Mesa and Escondido have tried to revitalize their downtowns but with uneven results. Placeless shopping malls and strip developments dominate much of the metropolitan region with little sense of a civic or even social nodality. Still, San Diego is probably better off than most large urban areas.

On the basis of Lynch's five elements of imageability, San Diego emerges as a relatively easy place around which to build a mental map. For a huge urban region, it makes sense as a place.

CHAPTER TWO

San Diego Realities: Social and Economic Trends

The images that define San Diego's metropolitan personality have some basis in fact, but they can sometimes take on a life of their own if not occasionally measured against current trends and data. In addition, recent figures from the 2000 census and studies done by local governments and economic organizations can help to flesh out the sometimes fuzzy images that have evolved over time. This chapter is as rich in data as the previous one was rich in legend. Together, they paint a reasonably good picture of what the San Diego region is like today.

SUN BELT BOOMTOWN OR MATURE METROPOLIS

The population of San Diego exploded during World War II and continued to grow rapidly for the next four decades. From just over 500,000 in 1950, the population grew to nearly 2,500,000 by 1990. San Diego's strong defense industry and fun in the sun image attracted hundreds of thousands of Americans from cooler climes. Since 1990, however, the rate of population growth has slowed. San Diego County's growth rate of 12.6 percent between

1990 and 2000 is well below that of current boomtowns such as Las Vegas (83 percent), Orlando (34 percent), or even Fresno (22 percent). In fact, it is below the levels posted by such Midwestern stalwarts as Indianapolis (16 percent) and Columbus, Ohio (14 percent).[1] Part of this reflects the economic downturn that affected all of California during the early 1990s, when cutbacks in defense spending sent people scurrying for better opportunities in nearby states. But there are other factors as well. In recent years, there has been a net out-migration of domestic residents, and only foreign immigrants and relatively high rates of natural increase have kept the population growing. Indeed, an excess of births over deaths currently accounts for twice as much growth as new in-migrants. At least some of this has to do with San Diego's extraordinarily high housing costs (median price over $440,000 in mid-2004, about twice the national average), making it one of the nation's least affordable areas. Businesses also face high land costs, taxes, and other significant costs for water and energy. Still, in 2002, San Diego County was estimated to have just over 2.9 million people and growing. One estimate predicts another one million people by 2020.

Geographic boundaries play a role in relative growth rates as well. San Diego has gone from being one of the largest metropolitan regions in area to one that is just about average for the U.S. While San Diego County is geographically huge compared to most of the counties in the United States, it is now and probably always will be the only county in the MSA. Indeed, the only possible addition is largely agricultural Imperial County in the desert to the east, which will likely be lightly inhabited for some time. Most other large metropolitan areas have grown in recent decades by adding nearby counties, as they become more connected by highways and more integrated into the economies of central cities. Atlanta, Houston, Minneapolis, and Seattle have added so many counties that these metropolitan areas are now as big or bigger in area than San Diego. These additions also serve to artificially inflate growth rates, since in many cases the population was already there but not counted in the metropolitan figures. Boston is an extreme case since the metropolitan Boston CMSA was created to include most of eastern Massachusetts and some parts of adjacent states. Most of these areas have been growing slowly if at all, but their recent inclusion in the metropolitan area nevertheless makes the population of greater Boston appear to be growing at nearly 7 percent. Atlanta is also an extreme case. Greater Atlanta now includes 20 counties and had a growth rate in the 1990s of 39 percent. But of course not all this growth is actually "growth" since it resulted from boundary changes.

While Atlanta, Minneapolis, Indianapolis, and Houston can easily spread out over the regional landscape, San Diego's growth potential is finite. San Diego, compared to many American metropolises, is running out of room. At the very most, about one-third of the county's acreage can be occupied by anything approaching urban or suburban densities, so about 1,200–1,500 square miles will probably be the maximum size of the urbanized area. This seems like a lot of space, but, given the hilly terrain, vast military bases, regional parks, and reservoirs within the "developable" area, options are even more limited.

San Diego is not alone. San Francisco, Los Angeles, and San Jose have also seen growth rates decline for many of the same reasons. Similarly, Boston, New York, Providence, Baltimore, New Orleans, and many other metropolitan areas now have difficulty finding room for the new space-extensive American lifestyle of megamalls, freeways, and grassy office parks. Limited land usually leads to high costs, and American developers are not fond of these.

On the other hand, limited space is not an entirely bad thing. Unlike many sprawling metropolises, the San Diego region has almost no abandoned houses or commercial buildings, and vacant lots are extremely rare in all built-up areas. Space is simply too valuable to remain underutilized. The retail outlook for San Diego, for example, is quite rosy compared to that of many Southern and Midwestern cities with unlimited land for expansion. The latter are more likely to experience serious overbuilding and abandonment. Maybe scarcity will lead to careful planning and real growth management. San Diego has begun this process, but it is still far behind leaders such as Portland, Oregon.[2]

In contrast to its popular image, San Diego, and indeed southern California in general, is not a low-density metropolis. National density figures are hard to interpret since cities and metropolitan areas vary so much in areal extent depending on annexation laws and county boundaries. Still, even with its nearly uninhabited mountains and deserts, metropolitan San Diego was situated in the middle of the pack in 1991 at 606 people per square mile. About 90 percent of the population live in the western quarter of the county, and so a reasonable figure for the urbanized region would be at least 2,500 people per square mile. Many parts of the urban area exhibit fairly high densities, with a few neighborhoods exceeding 30,000 people per square mile. Once again it is difficult to interpret the statistics since many San Diego neighborhoods are interlaced with canyons. Houses may be quite close together but the inclusion of green canyons in the neighborhood definition makes for lower overall density figures. Still, some realities are changing. Seventeen of the top forty densest cities in the U.S. in 2000 were California suburbs.[3]

San Diego County's population is increasingly both ethnically and economically diverse. As recently as the 1960s, San Diego was known for its "white bread" population. During the 1940s and 1950s, Anglo-Americans with names like Smith and Thompson flooded in from the South and Midwest and the minority population was very small. As mentioned earlier, only about 4 percent of the population was Latino in 1950 and the percentage for African Americans was similar. There were no large barrios or ghettos and even European ethnic districts were a rarity. Small clusters of Italians and Portuguese along the waterfront were all the region could muster.

In recent decades, not only has the population become much more ethnically diverse but the stage has been set for much greater diversity in the future. In the 2000 census, Hispanics made up 27 percent of the county's population, with 37 percent of those under age eighteen, double the white non-Hispanic percentage. Asians made up 9 percent of the population followed by blacks at 5 percent and Pacific Islanders, American Indians, and others making up 1 percent each. About 3 percent of the population claim to be of "two or more" races. This latter figure is of course grossly understated since many African Americans and Mexican Americans have evolved through a certain amount of "cultural interaction." The "other" category is increasingly diverse as well, with emerging Ethiopian, Somali, and Nigerian communities. The non-Hispanic white percentage in 2000 was 55 percent, and so there will soon be no "majority" population in the metropolitan region. This is especially true since many of the "whites" are immigrants from Russia, Eastern and Western Europe, and Iraq, and so make up a very internally diverse category. Since immigrants, especially Hispanics, tend to be young, a relative population explosion in the near future will lead to an ethnic polyglot that will be novel for twenty-first century San Diego. Several suburbs have higher ethnic percentages than the city, and so the metropolitan area as a whole and not just the "inner city" is experiencing these changes.

Of course, if Tijuana were officially part of the metropolitan region, its 1.5 million people would mean that the Greater San Diego-Tijuana area would be well over 50 percent Hispanic. As it is, the August 2002 edition of the magazine *Hispanic* declared San Diego to be the best city in the U.S. for Latinos.[4] The ranking was based not only on the usual things such as employment opportunities and quality of life but also on the presence of Hispanic cultural activities in both San Diego County and nearby Tijuana.

POLITICAL BOUNDARIES AND POLITICAL POWER

The City of San Diego has always covered a lot of territory. The original city boundary, derived from a Mexican land grant in 1850, was 74 square miles at a time when most American central cities were lucky to have 20. Significantly, some of the neighborhoods that would become San Diego's most desirable residential areas, such as La Jolla and Point Loma, were located in the original central city and so could not resist annexation attempts, as has often happened in elite neighborhoods elsewhere. Consequently, the San Diego region has never really been characterized by a poor central city surrounded by wealthy, politically independent suburbs. The socioeconomic status of city, suburbs, and unincorporated areas has been relatively evenly balanced compared to most American urban areas.

Over the years, the city of San Diego has annexed large hunks of territory and now encompasses 324 square miles with a population of 1.28 million. The "city," however, also includes vast agricultural preserves and even the sprawling Wild Animal Park. An important point here is that the large spatial extent and population of the central city colors nearly all comparative data, from average income and housing prices to crime rates and open space per capita. Since the city includes within its boundaries nearly every imaginable type of neighborhood from ranches to condos, as well as the complete gamut of ethnic and social groupings, it is very difficult to compare it with small central cities that have been unable to annex. At least half the new shopping malls and office parks in the San Diego region, for example, are in the city

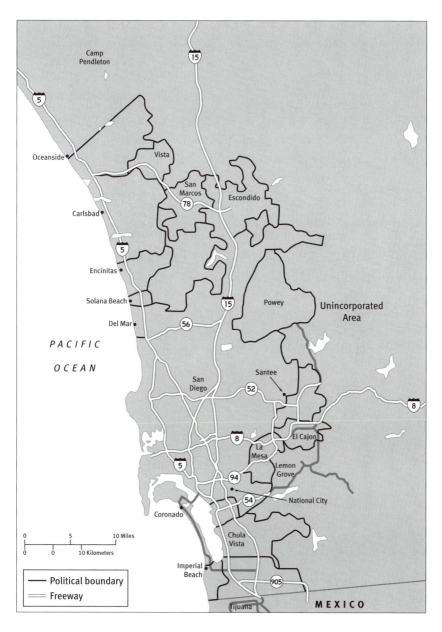

The incorporated cities and freeway system of San Diego County.

of San Diego. Similarly, many of the low income and/or ethnically diverse communities are outside the city. Comparing the city to, say, Newark or Cleveland is like comparing apples and oranges. The data are nearly meaningless unless the reader pays careful attention to the importance of boundaries and the size of the areal units. To a lesser but similar degree, comparisons of metropolitan regions are also difficult since there are likely to be wildly varying component territories. I include some data in this book, but they should be taken with a grain of salt.

The political organization of Metropolitan San Diego is becoming increasingly complex. As recently as 1970, there were only a few incorporated cities in the county and most people who did not live in San Diego proper lived in unincorporated areas. Today there are eighteen incorporated cities, many quite large and spatially extensive. At least three have over 150,000 people. In the year 2000, only about 440,000 people, about one-sixth of the population of the county, lived in unincorporated areas. Getting all the cities to cooperate in some form of regional government is a high priority on many political agendas.

The proliferation of cities has increased the difficulties involved in regional planning and the battle for new "turf" can lead to some rather weird political boundaries. An extreme example is the 40-foot-wide swath of water the city of San Diego annexed through San Diego Bay in order to acquire the border community of San Ysidro. Annexation battles sometimes lead to city boundaries that resemble doilies, with lace-like combinations of holes and extensions. In order to minimize conflicts, a Local Area Formation Commission (LAFCO) has been set up to rule on the feasibility of specific annexations. In addition, the San Diego Association of Governments (SANDAG), an umbrella organization to encourage cooperation between cities, has proven to be reasonably effective in the area of regional planning.

In addition to the county, individual cities, and SANDAG, there are a number of special districts that play important roles in the governance of the region. One that should be mentioned is the San Diego Unified Port District. The Port District controls all the land around San Diego Bay, more than twenty miles of shoreline, including the downtown San Diego waterfront, shipyards, marinas, tens of thousands of hotel rooms, and until recently the airport. The District's governing board is made up of representatives from the cities that line the Bay, but it is not elected and some have suggested that it is not always responsive to the public. One of its primary goals is to make money for the Port District so that further improvements can be carried out, such as dredging for new land creation and better ship channels, parks and amenities, and tourist attractions. No housing is permitted on Port land so the Bay is lined with convention facilities, hotels, shipyards, and other money-making operations. When the federal government, especially the military, is layered into the process, the levels of government can indeed be quite complex and decisions controversial.

The distribution of political power has also become more complex in recent years. San Diego was so well known for its ultraconservative politics that it is said that John F. Kennedy read the *San Diego Union* regularly to see what the other side was saying. Local politics were dominated by a good old boy network of old families, developers, military and ex-military leaders, and bankers well into the 1970s. Today there are a number of new players on the political scene.

In general, San Diego has become more moderate and occasionally even almost liberal. Not only is the Hispanic vote a factor to be reckoned with, but environmentalists have succeeded in mitigating at least some of the "growth at any cost" ideas of the traditional developer-backed leadership. Casinos on American Indian reservations have given that group enough money to wield considerable influence as well. Even labor, with 110,000 union members, has recently flexed its political muscle, something new in a region long known for its hostility to unions. The tourism industry is also bigger and more politically organized than ever and makes its presence felt in most elections. A generally well-educated segment of the population working in science and high-technology fields, as well as in local universities, also makes for more interesting political discussions, especially when allied with high-tech industry. In addition, the takeover of many local banks and corporations by outside companies has served to limit the power of traditional "bigwigs." Even though the war on terrorism has yet to pay big dividends to San Diego's defense-related in-dustries, the military vote remains important. All this has made for a more varied political climate than in years past. While San Diego County has sometimes voted for Democratic candidates in national elections, the local leadership tends to be Republican.

A MYSTERIOUSLY STRONG ECONOMY

The May 2002 edition of *Forbes Magazine* rated San Diego first among 200 metropolitan areas in the country for business and careers.[5] San Diego led the California rebound (six of the top ten were in the Golden State) from the doldrums of the early 1990s with a job growth rate of 21 percent. The magazine praised the fact that San Diego's diverse economy is able to weather eco-nomic cycles such as the dotcom debacle and, it appears, even drastic declines in defense spending. San Diego has "a mix of strong companies within a broad technology base" that includes Sempra Energy, Qualcomm, IDEC Pharmaceuticals, and nearly 500 biotech firms. This, in combination with a strong tourist in-dustry, a maquiladora-centered border economy, a large number of high quality educational institutions, and a diverse service in-dustry moved San Diego up from eighth place in 2001. Given the doldrums that have beset many San Diego companies of late, the ranking could mean that the region is simply the best of a bad lot. Things have slowed from the boom years of the late 1990s, but there is still a great deal of optimisim. The Big Four components of economic growth in the county in order of importance are manufacturing (especially high-tech), defense, tourism, and agriculture.

Of course these rankings must be taken with a grain of salt since a particular city can rise and fall with great speed during economic adjustments. San Francisco fell from first to fifty-fourth in the Forbes survey in one year with the dot.com crisis, and Seattle plummeted from fifteenth to ninety-second. Still, San Diego seems to have held its own during the 2003–4 downturn despite its longer history of periodic booms and busts. Although San Diego's economy is still strong according to the 2002 criteria, Forbes added some new variables including the cost of doing business for its 2003 report. As expected, high cost cities such as Boston and San Diego fared poorly in comparison with places like Austin (no. 1) and Boise (no. 2). Still, San Diego ranked twenty-seventh, with mostly small, inexpensive cities rated higher.[6] The 2002 and 2003 rankings are just one magazine's opinion, but they do merit some discussion.

At first glance, the economic strength of San Diego is a bit mysterious since it lacks many of the factors traditionally associated with an economic powerhouse. The region has no significant raw materials and must import nearly everything it uses from far away, including water and lumber. It also has very poor transportation connections with few ways to get out of town. The only rail route is north to Los Angeles and (the very congested) freeways only lead to the metropolis to the north, the desert to the east and the Mexican border to the South. The airport is small for a metropolitan area the size of San Diego, ranking about twenty-sixth in the U.S. in passengers served, but well below the larger airports in absolute numbers. Most flights must pass through a major hub somewhere. The port handles very little tonnage since San Diego has few bulk exports. Exported products include computers and other electronic equipment, medical instruments, and cellular phones. These things do not fill large ships, especially since the main destination is Mexico. The quantity and bulk of imports, however, are improving. Dole uses the Tenth Avenue Terminal to import up to 600,000 metric tons of fruit each year, and automobiles and lumber are imported through the National City Terminal. But San Diego is not poised to become a distribution center for an extended region or hinterland, and ships have a hard time finding materials to carry away from the city.

Neither is San Diego a central place. Unlike Denver, Atlanta, Minneapolis, or Seattle, it is not an all-purpose center for a large and diverse section of the country. The cities just mentioned, for example, are the media, wholesale, and distribution centers for the smaller towns and cities for hundreds of miles around. San Diego has no such region to serve. Squeezed between Los Angeles and Mexico, its central place functions are minimal. No one reads the San Diego newspaper, follows San Diego sports teams, or watches San Diego television stations except San Diegans. Partly as a result, sports teams have been noticeably fickle. Basketball has departed entirely after several tries, and the city struggles to keep pro football by buying up unsold tickets for each game, costing taxpayers millions of dollars. The combined populations of San Diego and Tijuana provide a sizable market for service industries but nothing comparable to, say, Atlanta or Dallas/Fort Worth. This is especially true since northern Mexico has a much lower per capita buying power.

The costs of land, energy, water, and most other things from license plates to gasoline are relatively high. The average rent for an apartment surpasses $1,100 per month, $300–400 more than in similar sized metropolitan areas in the Midwest and South. At the same time, the large number of people employed in the low-paid end of the service industry, such as hotel maids, waiters, tour bus operators, and retail clerks, means that there is a serious housing crunch. The size of the average household is increasing as many people double up.

San Diego is also not a major center for corporate headquarters. There are relatively few large employers in the San Diego area other than the usual candidates like the San Diego Unified School District, major hospitals and universities, and the city and county of San Diego, along with a few more atypical ones such as military bases and Sea World. No major banks, insurance companies or other financial institutions are headquartered in San Diego any longer, though some have been bought up and merged. Among the reasonably large corporate headquarters are Qualcomm (telecommunications), the largest, with about 7,000 employees, and Sempra Energy, Titan Corporation, National Steel and Shipbuilding, Jack in the Box restaurants, and Calloway Golf Company. The high-tech sector gets most of the press, with communication, computer and electronics, and biotechnology and pharmaceuticals each having about 24,000 employees in 2002.[7] But other trends are occurring. The rapidly growing number of Indian gaming casinos have a work force of over 12,000 and may soon be one of the biggest single types of employment. The vast majority of firms are either very small or are branches of corporations headquartered elsewhere such as Sony and Hewlett-Packard. Thus there are few big decision makers in San Diego, and some have argued that the region lacks the kind of leadership associated, for example, with the Mellons in Pittsburgh, the Fords in Detroit, or Bill Gates in Seattle.

To a very real degree, the fate of San Diego is often decided elsewhere. This happened in the 1980s when the Navy decided to build a new hospital in the middle of Balboa Park despite opposition by much of the elected leadership. The military has played a major role in shaping the San Diego landscape, but the decisions are usually made in Washington. Similar stories can be told about local companies taken over by outsiders and then closed, as happened when Convair was absorbed by General Dynamics.

On the other hand, the fact that San Diego has many small employers rather than a few big ones means that it can often roll with the punches and avoid the major crises that can occur when a corporate giant gets into trouble. As it is, the Navy and its associated contractors provide some stability while new, entrepreneurial companies come and go around the edges. At the present time, this model seems to be working. Still, there is a tendency for small, often undercapitalized San Diego companies either to fail or succeed and be taken over (like the Rohr Corporation, now BF Goodrich) by larger outside corporations.

Another mysterious aspect of the San Diego economy is agriculture. In many urban areas, agriculture declines as "higher and better" urban land uses push farmers off the land. In the San Diego area, however, high value agriculture has been booming even in the face of outrageously high land and water costs. The biggest gainers, as noted earlier, are horticulture on the one hand and avocados on the other. Cut flowers and nursery crops accounted for 66 percent of the value of all agriculture in 2001 and posted an 8.5 percent increase over the previous year. Citrus, vegetables, eggs, tomatos, and other products have been holding on or declining slightly due to foreign competition. Still, agricultural production has increased every year over the past decade and is now valued at $1.3 billion.[8] Most of the 6,000 farms in the county are small, family owned operations with an average age of farmers of about sixty, so it is difficult to say how long prosperity will linger as urbanization increases. The demand for cut flowers in nearby Los Angeles and indeed the world is high, however, and so the end may not come soon.

And so, as we examine the mysterious economy, two traditional components, defense and agriculture, seem destined to thrive for at least the near future. The Navy is committed to San Diego and despite cutbacks remains an important economic "anchor," along with, ironically, flowers. The number of military personnel in San Diego at any given time varies but normally exceeds 100,000 people. The military has also spun off a large cast of supporting industries over the decades. Even though the aerospace industry has declined, a large number of defense-related industries still exist. The region holds a national "megaport" designation by the Navy and is one of the few places where large Navy vessels can be maintained. It is also the site of the Space and Naval Warfare Systems Command (SPAWAR), with its annual operating budget of four billion dollars for developing information technologies. San Diego has about 140 firms in the defense and space cluster employing about 19,000 people. Examples include Science Applications International Corporation, National Steel and Shipbuilding, BFGoodrich Aerospace Aerostructures Groups, Cubic, and General Atomics.[9]

Tourism has remained strong as well despite ebbs and flows with economic cycles and fears of terrorism. San Diego's location just south of a huge metropolitan area with over ten million people translates into a large potential market for weekend tourists heading for the beaches and the zoo. The extraordinary growth of inland cities such as Phoenix and Las Vegas created thousands of people seeking cooler sites closer to the ocean, at least during the sizzling summer months. Until recently, the increasing affluence of Asian countries like Japan and Taiwan guaranteed a steady source of foreign tourists to complement those from Canada, Europe, and Latin America. Given its climate and attractions, San Diego's tourist industry is likely to remain strong even with its relatively small airport and remote location. Daily shoppers and "tourists" from Baja California are also important since, as mentioned earlier, they are not officially part of the metropolitan area and so bring in money from the outside. With the opening and subsequent expansion of a huge downtown convention center during the 1990s, the region has also become a major destination for business and professional travel. In the year 2000, there were over fifteen million overnight visitors to San Diego adding about five billion dollars to the local economy.[10]

The main source of economic mystery revolves around manufacturing, the number one basic industry and source of income for the San Diego economy. With high-tech manufacturing beginning to exhibit some of the same fragility that has affected heavy industry for the last few decades, it is useful to ponder just what keeps San Diego going. Given the sub-optimal location and infrastructure for manufacturing, there are three major explanations for the success of this sector in recent years—plentiful jobs and qualified employees at the high end, plentiful jobs and employees at the low end, and a growth breeds growth mentality.

Most of the attention has gone to the first of these factors. San Diego's diverse economy has become famous for its highly educated, very productive, and appropriately skilled workforce. In 1998, about 122,000 workers were employed in San Diego's high-tech industries. San Diego usually ranks high among large American metropolitan economies in productivity per worker, university research and development per worker, patents per worker, early stage venture capital, exports, and gross metro product growth.[11] These high marks resulted from San Diego's success in manufacturing small, high value products such as medical instruments, cell phones, and sophisticated electronic equipment. The presence of a highly skilled San Diego workforce results from at least three factors. First, the demise of the aerospace industry meant that for a time there were a large number of unemployed engineers and other skilled workers in San Diego, and many sought to create new firms rather than leave the area in search of increasingly fickle large employers. This resulted in a cadre of entrepreneurial engineers and a boom in small firms of many different kinds.

The second factor is the abundance of universities and research institutes in Southern California with emphasis on some combination of biological, engineering, and business expertise. The University of California, San Diego and San Diego State University each provide thousands of skilled graduates every year, as do the many other universities in nearby metropolitan areas such as Orange County and Los Angeles, including UC Irvine, UCLA, and Cal Tech. In addition, research facilities such as Scripps Institute of Oceanography, Scripps Research Institute, Salk Institute, San Diego Supercomputer, International Thermonuclear Experimental Reactor Project, and Hubbs-Seaworld Research Institute play a role. The major symbiotic relationship between universities and major hospitals is important in many metropolitan areas, and it certainly fits San Diego as well.

The third factor is ambience. The climate, topography, image, and landscape of San Diego attract mobile people from all over the country, among them doctors, scientists, inventors, and entrepreneurs. These highly paid professionals do not even worry about outrageous housing prices, perhaps viewing these as wise investment opportunities. This attraction to San Diego is higher because of the Navy. Over the decades, thousands of military personnel have passed through the area and vowed to return someday. "I remember when I was stationed there" is a common phrase that comes up when discussing San Diego with people all around the U.S.

These factors help explain the large number of patents per worker, but they do not explain all aspects of worker productivity. For that, we must look at the jobs at the low end of the spectrum. In the study of fifteen metropolitan areas mentioned above, San Diego was ranked near the bottom in the ratio between high quality jobs created and overall job growth.[12] It was also rated below average in real estate construction per capita. This means that in addition to the highly skilled professionals discussed above, San Diego is home to a growing mass of relatively low skill, low paid workers who are increasingly crammed into small spaces both at home and at work. There is, however, an important symbiotic relationship here.

The quality of life for the wealthy in San Diego is enhanced by the abundance of low cost labor that has resulted from high rates of legal and illegal foreign immigration. Service occupations, such as maids, gardeners, car and home repair, tree removal, cab driving, cooks, waiters, and many types of retail are dominated by foreign, especially Latino workers. It can be argued, for example, that for those interested in "starting up" a small company, the abundance of eager, hard working, low paid, and usually reliable employees is a plus. Those with "iffy" status with the INS are also relatively docile and uncomplaining. This is, of course, a matter for concern, since social and economic bifurcation between rich and poor is making the region more like a Third World metropolis than an ideal place to live.[13]

But there is some "voluntary exploitation" as well. A large number of young native San Diegans offer their labor to ad hoc employers in order to stay in what they perceive to be a place with ideal surfing and rock climbing. Some of these eventually become entrepreneurs and start their own small company. It is not a region that young people tend to leave eagerly in search of greener pastures.

A major source of low paid labor in recent decades has been the maquiladoras on the Mexican side of the border.[14] Beginning during the labor shortages of World War II and lasting until 1963, the Bracero Program allowed Mexicans to cross the border easily as "guest workers" for employment. Most of this employment was in agriculture as few Americans were available or interested in work as fruit pickers. After the program was canceled, Mexico sought to diversify its border economy with a Mexican Border Industrialization Program in order to provide jobs for its booming northern population. The result was maquiladora industries, factories that were partially or wholly foreign owned located in a border free-trade zone. Materials and semifinished products could be imported for labor-intensive manufacturing operations and then exported to the market (chiefly the U.S.) with no duties or state taxes involved. In addition, management could work in Mexico without paying income taxes if they were on the payroll of a participating foreign company. American companies could thus locate in southern California (or Texas, and so on) and use low-cost Mexican labor. Female labor was especially important, whether because women tended to be more facile with tiny, detailed components such as those used in electronics or because they were cheaper and more docile than males, depending on what side of the political spectrum you ask.

The program grew slowly during the 1970s, in part because labor was cheaper in many other foreign countries, especially Asia, than in Mexico. With the collapse of the Mexican economy and the devaluation of the peso in 1982, factories on the border became much more competitive and the maquiladoras boomed with growth rates of 20 percent per year from 1984 to 1990. Growth slowed in the 1990s but still normally exceeded 10 percent per year. In Tijuana, the maquiladora industry peaked in early 2001 with 820 plants employing 194,500 people. A year later, there were 712 plants employing 145,900 people.

Ironically, the decline in maquiladoras is at least partly the result of the North American Free Trade Agreement (NAFTA) and the increasing importance of international trade within the North American continent. NAFTA went into effect in 1994 and requires that a growing number of manufactured products be exempt from all tariffs. By the time it is fully phased in, virtually all goods manufactured in the three countries will be traded duty free.

There will no longer be a need for a special zone at the border and so plants located in the Mexican interior will have increasing importance. Access to the U.S. market will still be of value, but Mexico will need to rely on more than cheap labor to attract industries to places like Tijuana. Infrastructures will have to be upgraded and skill levels increased. The ball is in the Mexican court. To make matters even more problematic, very low wage countries like China and India are attracting more investment than ever in the age of globalization. It remains to be seen whether the gradual demise of border industries will lead to increasing illegal immigration and a glut of low cost labor on the U.S. side of the border.

A final dimension of San Diego's economy that is worth mentioning is what I call "growth breeds growth," a kind of snowball effect that has been very common throughout the history of urbanization in North America. San Diego, like much of southern California, has experienced boom and bust times over the past century and a half. During the boom times, at least, unbridled optimisim has prevailed and money has flowed like water into nearly every kind of investment opportunity from land and housing to new businesses such as restaurants, hotels, and shopping centers. New residents mean new markets and so construction, as well as construction loans, etc., have been a major source of employment. On the other hand, when busts have occurred, they have sometimes been severe. San Diego's economy collapsed several times between the late 1880s and the early 1960s. The early 1990s also brought a major downturn. Image and perception have played important roles in shaping the local economic scene.

The same mentality has prevailed as well in specialized sectors of the local economy. When aerospace was booming it really boomed, but when it started down it crashed in a hurry. Today, there is trouble on the horizon for the much-vaunted high-tech world. Gateway Computers and Peregrine Systems suffered severe losses in early 2002 and the prospect for new firms is not as bright as it once was. A new telecommunications company, Leap, which specializes in bargain cellular phone networks, has had trouble getting off the ground. Even some biotech products such as Metabolife have come under fire (in this case for using the controversial herbal supplement ephedrine in its diet product), making "one drug wonder" companies appear more vulnerable than before. These problems will probably not result in a "bust" this time, but growth that has resulted from an uncompromising boom mentality may diminish.

THE PHYSICAL ENVIRONMENT: ATTRIBUTES, PROBLEMS, AND CONSTRAINTS

When people think of San Diego's physical environment, the two things that most often come to mind are probably ideal climate and earthquakes. San Diego does have its faults, although the fearsome San Andreas lies well to the east of the heavily populated area. So far a major earthquake has not damaged San Diego but, to people back east especially, San Diegans are seen as playing gleefully in the sun as the whole state of California prepares to slide into the Pacific Ocean. While this perception may not be incorrect, the most immediate environmental issues facing San Diegans usually involve water, both too little and too much of it. Droughts, fires, and floods have been the major constraints to life in San Diego and the major causes of death and destruction. To understand this, let us examine the region's physical setting in greater detail.

It is difficult to talk about the climate of San Diego, since the county contains no fewer than five of the world's major climatic zonal types or ecological zones. When someone says that San Diego has the best climate in the U.S., therefore, the appropriate

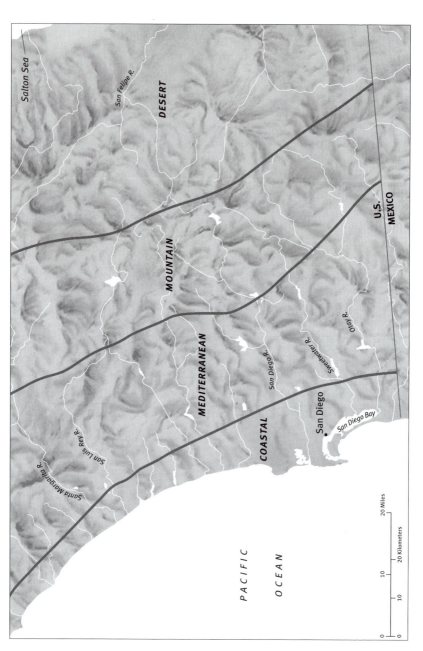

Physical geography and climate zones of the San Diego area.

response might be to ask exactly what part of the metropolitan area is being discussed. The climate zones are arranged in north-south strips starting at the coast. The coastal climate, so often referred to as Mediterranean, is actually, at least according to the Koppen system, semi-arid, cool. Most parts of the coast get less than 9 inches of rain per year and are best classified as a steppe climate. It would seem very dry indeed without the on shore flow of marine air and fog that results from the cool currents coming down from the North Pacific.

Further inland and uphill, the climate becomes "Mediterranean, hot summer." This zone extends from the eastern suburbs of San Diego to the inland foothills and agricultural valleys. Interestingly, just about at the point where a Mediterranean climate actually begins, the Mediterranean landscape of Spanish architecture and vegetation ends and the rustic western look begins. These areas usually experience about 12–15 inches of rain annually. Higher still, we encounter Mediterranean, cool summer, in the (6,000-plus-foot) mountain peaks. Some areas in this zone may receive almost 50 inches of rain as well as substantial amounts of snow per year. East of the mountains, there are two more climatic zones, semi-arid, hot and arid or desert. The desert may get only 1 or 2 inches of precipitation a year, sometimes all in one storm. Obviously, temperatures and vegetation vary within these ecological zones as well, with summer high temperatures on the coast often 40 degrees F cooler than those in the desert. What is the San Diego climate? What does the landscape look like?

The operative word in describing all these climate zones is "average," especially with regard to rainfall, since very few years actually bring an average amount to any part of the metropolitan region. Rainfall in San Diego County is extremely variable from year to year. In the city of San Diego, where rainfall is measured at Lindbergh Field near the coast, annual rainfall has varied from less than 3.5 inches to 26 inches over the past 115 years.[15] The year 2001–2 was at or close to a new low and wells are going dry in the eastern foothills. The year 2003–4 may be even drier. Rainfall is also highly seasonal, with about 85 percent occurring between the months of October and April. Even during these "wet" months, however, the rain can come in one intense downpour followed by weeks of none at all. Streams tend to be either dry or flooded, making for some difficult planning decisions. During a long series of dry years, for example, homes and businesses have often been built in areas that flood during wet years. When the wet years come, shopping centers, theaters, and warehouses are underwater while houses slide off their hillside perches. So far, San Diego has avoided Los Angeles-style concrete flood channels in favor of dredging more "natural-looking" watercourses. Still, flooding remains a major hazard in sunny San Diego.

It should be mentioned that not all excess water problems are a result of precipitation. The combination of high winds and high tides often causes severe beach erosion, and a few nineteenth-century neighborhoods have virtually disappeared into the ocean. Flooding in the community of Mission Beach is usually the result of waves washing over the sea wall and backing up in the storm drains. When heavy rains and high tides come together, the dangers increase, and many seaside cliffs have been lined with controversial riprap or piles of large concrete blocks. Indeed, the picturesque cliffs that face the ocean in such desirable neighborhoods as La Jolla are all the result of wave erosion. The problem has increased as dams upstream have limited the new sand deposits along the coast.

In spite of occasional flood dangers, most of the time the problem is too little water rather than too much. San Diego is about 90 percent dependent on imported water, and this will no doubt increase in the future since there are few places for new dams. The last local reservoirs were completed in the early 1950s, and even these are less than ideal as dependable sources of water. Local reservoirs are less than half full during most years as precipitation is either scant or absorbed by the parched ground. As the populations of Arizona and Nevada increase, the political conflicts over water supplies such as the Colorado River can only become more intense. Even normally moist Northern California resents the exportation of water to the south during dry years. During the drought of 2002, deals were cut with the farmers of Imperial County to limit production and ship more water to San Diego, but this was probably a short-term solution.

At present, most of San Diego's water is a mixture of water from the Colorado River and from Northern California with about two-thirds coming from the former. New aqueducts are under construction and there is talk about desalinization but demand is rapidly increasing as well. Conservation measures have been pushed and xerophytic (drought-resistant) vegetation has replaced grass lawns here and there, but the county still uses about 700,000 acre feet of water per year.

The view from the air says it all. The U.S.-Mexican border stands out not only because of the differences in land use, architecture, and street morphology, but because of what seems to be an entirely different climate. The U.S. appears green and Mexico tan. The difference, of course, results from the heavy use of imported water and irrigation on the northern side of the line. Without imported water, the idyllic Mediterranean landscape of San Diego would be impossible to maintain. With nearly 60 percent of San Diego's water used by residential households, the typical domestic landscape and lifestyle is vulnerable to water shortages. In the not-too-distant future, San Diego may look as tan as Tijuana and the image of the city may change as its color fades.

Droughts have the greatest impact on the backcountry in San Diego County. The chaparral vegetation becomes extremely dry after a year or so with minimal rain and fires are almost the norm.

Fires can be the result of lightning or human negligence and are very difficult to control when hot winds are blowing. In 1970, for example, the Laguna Fire burned 175,000 acres and destroyed many properties in suburban San Diego. In the summer of 2002, another fire burned 66,000 acres, destroyed over 100 structures, and threatened several new, upscale rancho developments in the mountains. Ironically, heavy rains in one year often lead to terrible fires in another since the vegetation grows thicker in wet years only to provide more fuel when it dries out. Fires occur in the city as well. In 1985, a fire on a steep hillside destroyed dozens of homes near the center of San Diego. The physical environment in San Diego is not quite as benign as its idyllic image might suggest. As a draft of this book was being written in 2003, the largest fire ever recorded in California was blazing away not far from my office. Dubbed the Cedar Fire, it quickly burned over 300,000 acres and destroyed over 2,200 homes and 2,000 other structures. Three other large fires were burning in San Diego County during the same period along with several more in the Los Angeles area. Smoke and ash filled the air in every direction. At this point, the physical environment is not widely viewed as benign. Indeed, the 2003 fires damaged three of the case study communities covered in this book while another was seriously threatened. I will cover this topic in greater detail in Chapter 5 under the topic of mountain towns such as Julian.

While fires and floods have been consistently unwelcome constraints to growth in San Diego, the impact of the complex topography has been more difficult to gauge. San Diego Bay is nearly surrounded by a narrow, flat plain that has been above water for only a few thousand years. Most of the coastal region, however, consists of dissected marine terraces, commonly referred to as mesas. These relatively flat tablelands are separated one from another by steep canyons and river valleys. Further inland, hills and small mountains interspersed with modest valleys become more common. Finally, the high mountains of the Peninsular Range give way to the below sea level Salton Trough in the desert. This complex topography has been both a major attraction and a difficult constraint for development in San Diego.

The social and economic geography of the region has been at least partly shaped by topography. It is commonly said, for example, that wherever there is a notable hill, there are rich people on top. Wealthy neighborhood names often include a physical description such as Mount Soledad, Mount Helix, or Del Cerro. As a result, San Diego exhibits a fair degree of socioeconomic mixing at the neighborhood scale. A variety of communities have mansions on the hills with modest houses and apartments down slope. There are also many places where busy gas stations and strip malls coexist with nearby peaceful and charming residential areas due to a difference in elevation of perhaps 50–100 feet. In addition, neighborhood identity and sense of place are enhanced by the fact that each one is separated from the next by an intervening canyon. This is very different from the situation on the Los Angeles Plain, where long, straight streets go on uninterrupted for ten or twenty miles. In San Diego, people seek out not only the location but also the elevation that they desire and can afford. Difficult topography can add to the interest, charm, and views of a neighborhood, but it can also add to the cost of housing. As the easily developed areas have been taken, new housing construction increasingly involves sluicing hillsides or expensive grading. Much of it is controversial if not downright ugly.

Topography has been an even more important constraint for commercial and industrial development. The scarcity of good sites for retail and industrial facilities is partly due to the scarcity of easily developable land. The city of El Cajon typifies the kind of land use assemblages in many parts of the county. El Cajon ("box" in Spanish) is made up of a flat valley surrounded by hills. The central lowland contains virtually all the commercial and in-

The view east toward the desert from Mount Laguna at 6,000 feet.

dustrial space as well as many large apartment complexes. The hills are covered with middle to high end single-family homes. While the physical setting did not strictly determine land use, it would have been difficult to have a very different pattern. But San Diego may be running out of such boxes, and new industrial complexes such as those on the edge of the booming Sorrento Valley near La Jolla require extensive grading and earth moving that only affluent high-tech firms can afford.

The constraints provided by topography and flood dangers are joined in San Diego by environmental restrictions in a large number of settings. Because of its climate and physical diversity, San Diego County has a greater variety of species, as well as more endangered species, than any other county in the U.S.[16] Several areas have been set aside to preserve what is left of the "natural" environment. While this is not unique to San Diego, these parks and preserves are much larger than those in most metropolitan areas. Cleveland National Forest, for example, contains over 288,000 acres, and Anza-Borrego Desert State Park 522,000 acres (472,000 in San Diego County), together about 117 square miles. And there are many others. The city of San Diego alone has well over 20,000 acres in parks and preserves. While most are intended for recreation, others are focused on protecting rare and endangered species. Where rivers enter the ocean, for example, there are usually marshy lagoons that provide habitats for plants and creatures not commonly found in the region. Development must skirt these beachfront preserves. Nature parks often figure strongly in community sense of place. They are major attractions, but they also serve to channel and direct development.

The physical environment in San Diego is especially problematic when it comes to transportation. Typically, freeways and other major highways follow canyons and other low-lying corridors. Thus highways as well as topographic features often separate individual neighborhoods. Cliffs and hillsides present serious challenges to road builders because of their steepness and the probability of erosion problems. The dissected plateaus of San Diego are even more difficult to connect with streets than the hills of San Francisco. As a result, there are a limited number of through streets in most areas. Unlike the typical midwestern city or even Los Angeles, there are few extensive grids offering multiple routes in every direction. Traffic must be channeled onto a few major thoroughfares.

The problem is well illustrated by the freeway network. There are essentially only two ways to get from San Diego to Los Angeles, Interstates 5 and 15. There are no through country roads. Similarly, Interstate 8 is the only feasible route to Arizona. As the communities to the north and east of San Diego are built up, traffic increases on the only paths available, sometimes to intolerable levels. Of course, major shopping centers and office parks are usually built along these few routes making for even more congestion. So far, the only solution has been to widen the freeways and to add bus and carpool lanes but that cannot go on forever as many sections already have six lanes in each direction. Topography has tended to increase the prevalence of cul-de-sac and "loop and lollipop" street patterns since mesas and valleys often have only one access road. The isolation of individual neighborhoods leads to even more automobile trips, as people must drive fairly long distances just to get out of the loop. The popularity of gated enclaves further segments the population into isolated clusters.

San Diego has a light rail system with three lines leading out of downtown San Diego. These too follow low-lying paths of least resistance generally paralleling existing freeways. The result, when completed, will be an even more linear pattern of commercial development.

SUSTAINABLE CITY OR TEMPORARY PARADISE

In 1974, Hamilton Marston, the patriarch of one of San Diego's oldest families, brought in urban planners Kevin Lynch and Donald Appleyard from MIT in Boston to evaluate the various trends in the rapidly growing region and make some recommendations. The result was a publication called *Temporary Paradise: A Look at the Special Landscape of the San Diego Region.*[17] The 52-page study was produced in newspaper format and distributed free throughout San Diego. For a while, it seemed like everyone had a copy and you could even find them in restroom stalls. Lynch and Appleyard, as the title suggests, were concerned about many of the trends impacting the metropolitan area during the early 1970s, even though the region had only about half as many people as it does today. They argued that San Diegans would have to manage the region carefully if they wanted it to remain an idyllic paradise. They stated, "The city's magnificent site, for which its citizens have such strong affection, is still intact, but may be losing its best qualities." Many of the suggestions in the report are based on fairly standard "good planning" ideas such as more bike paths, transit oriented development, and architectural conservation. Others are more region-specific and have to do with creating ecological preserves in the finger canyons and making use of modern versions of Spanish courtyard houses and patios rather than water-intensive front lawns. *Temporary Paradise* is filled with sketches, mental maps, architectural drawings, and a variety of intriguing low cost visuals.

It is hard to say what the impact of the report actually was. Certainly many people became aware for the first time that San Diego was importing many of the worst standard practices and designs from American cities elsewhere and was thus in the process of losing much of its character and identity. Many of these people were important planners and business leaders in the region. On the other hand, some changes for the better were afoot everywhere in America at the time and were part of a larger awareness and context. For example, the Bicentennial helped to publicize the importance of historic preservation while the advent of Earth Day brought a greater awareness of environmental degradation. The worst excesses of bland, drive-in modern architecture were over and the popularity of venues for the arts was increasing. San Diego probably became more enlightened as a result of the study, but rampant growth in subsequent years made it difficult to always pay attention to quality of life issues. Some of the passion created during the Earth Day decade has waned even as some of the worst air and water pollution problems have diminished. But today, new crises loom on the horizon and the public is well aware of most of them.

In the summer of 2002, SANDAG, the San Diego Association of Governments, put out a new and quite detailed study entitled *Indicators of Sustainable Competitiveness: San Diego Region.*[18]

The 140-page report compared the San Diego region with twenty other metropolitan areas of similar size as well as with the U.S. metropolitan average in order to see if San Diego's prosperity was sustainable in the face of increasing competition. In addition, the report focused on trends to see if San Diego was improving in absolute as well as relative terms. Data were collected in four categories; economic, environment, equity, and overall balance. The report indicates that the region is generally doing very well but its success is uneven. In overall sustainable competitiveness, San Diego ranked ninth out of twenty-one, with Austin, Raleigh, and Minneapolis leading the pack and Miami, Phoenix, and Tampa at the bottom. San Diego ranked third in the environmental area, tenth in economic, twelfth in balance, and nineteenth in equity. The latter topic is clearly worrisome.

In the environmental category, San Diego appeared quite strong; this is positive, given the region's dependence on being perceived as an attractive and healthy place to be. Although it was below average in air quality and capital outlays for solid waste disposal, higher rankings in water quality, water utilities, crime, and sewerage pulled the overall rating up to third, just behind Austin and Denver, with Boston and Washington, D.C. at the bottom. Of course, while San Diego has made progress in the environmental area, the problems associated with its clean-up have not been as substantial as those in, say, Pittsburgh or Baltimore. It is not now and never has been a center of heavy industry with many brown-field sites. Still, there have been some unique problems, such as the Navy being largely excluded from basic environmental regulations and the sewage outfall from Tijuana affecting the beaches of South County. In spite of some well-publicized beach closings resulting from street runoff during heavy rains, San Diego's primary environmental concern for the future is simply finding enough water.

In the economic category, San Diego ranks tenth in the study with San Francisco and San Jose leading the pack and Norfolk and Miami bringing up the rear. The relevant data and standings, however, are constantly changing, and some of the bloom may have gone off Silicon Valley since the report was initiated. The list of economic components examined is a long one and includes such things as per capita income, job growth, patents, unemployment rate, exports, capital outlays for air transport and highways, and education levels. As discussed, San Diego ranks very high as a center for innovation, patents, and venture capital. It is also busily improving its infrastructure, although there may be limits to the growth of the airport and the number of possible new highways. Per capita income is above the U.S. average, but the gap has narrowed over the past decade and the region ranks only sixteenth in the study. The major problem is that San Diego continues to add jobs in low paying industries at a faster rate than in high paying ones. In addition, the remuneration at the high end may well decrease for a while since during the 1990s, much of the income in the high-tech cluster came in the form of stock options. Trends in the economic world are changing rapidly in the early 2000s. Already, the amount of venture capital coming to San Diego has declined dramatically but with the "war on terrorism" expenditures in the defense industry may well increase.

San Diego is also bipolar in education, with the number of people with advanced degrees increasing along with those who lack a high school diploma. This does not bode well for long-term economic growth, especially in the high-tech sector. Children are not doing that well either. In the category "percentage of children in pre-school," for example, San Diego ranks eighteenth.

The major regional shortcoming in San Diego revolves around the issue of the social issue of rich and poor. It ranks nineteenth among the twenty-one metropolitan areas in the equity category. The main culprits are the divergent trend in income distribution discussed above and the cost of housing. San Diego is booming at both ends of the payroll spectrum, with increases in both the well paid and low paid at the expense of the middle-income group. The latter decreased from 46 percent of the population to 35 percent during the 1990s. Meanwhile, the cost of housing has exploded, increasing by over 25 percent from 2001 to 2002. The median price of a house was $333,000 in mid-2002, climbing to over $400,000 by early 2004. Average rent exceeds $1,200. Homeownership rates are well below the U.S. average at about 55 percent, and even this figure is somewhat misleading since it often means that people bought something they could not afford simply because they were desperate to get into the market. Only San Francisco and San Jose rank below San Diego in housing affordability.

It is estimated that at least 150,000 people commute to jobs in San Diego from Riverside County or Mexico because of the high price of local housing. To complicate the matter, San Diego is seen by some wealthy individuals as a desirable place to dump money. Mysterious, anonymous buyers occasionally make the news by paying $25 million in cash for a beach house, sometimes with the aim of tearing it down to build a better one. Millionaires from all over the country buy luxury condominiums or estates in gated communities that they intend to occupy only part of the year. San Diego is a delightful setting but it is also a good place to invest.

San Diego also does relatively poorly (fourteenth) in the category of health care. This is ironic since the high-tech realm in which the region gets the most patents involves drugs, pharmaceuticals, medical instruments, and other health related areas. Still, San Diego ranks fourteenth in hospital beds per capita, and about 22 percent of the population do not have any form of health insurance. The region also does not do well on measures of highway congestion or capital outlays for public transit, although average commute times are not excessive.

In terms of balance, San Diego ranks in the middle of the pack in eleventh place. Interestingly, San Francisco and Norfolk rank at the bottom for different reasons: San Francisco is very strong in economics but bad in equity, while the opposite is true in Norfolk. Raleigh is at the top as the most balanced metropolitan area.

CONTINUITY AND CHANGE

San Diego has changed in many ways over the past few decades. It has gone from a blue-collar, middle-class small town dominated by sailors, retirees, aerospace workers, shipbuilders, and shop-keepers to a sprawling metropolis increasingly polarized with high-tech computer jockeys and Mexican gardeners. The political leadership no longer contains the old assemblage of bankers, re-tailers, ranchers, and retired military but is increasingly driven by software gurus and telecommunication wizards. The urban area has gone from having an overwhelmingly White Anglo population to being one of the most ethnically diverse metropolitan regions in the country. While overall population densities have decreased due to rampant suburban sprawl, many neighborhoods have been built up to the point of looking very much like the older cities of the East Coast. In terms of freeways, shopping malls, housing tracts, office and industrial parks, and nondescript commercial strips, San Diego has become more like a normal American metro-politan area over the past few decades. The pace and quality of life have changed in many ways, sometimes for the better and sometimes for the worse. Still, San Diego has retained a strong sense of place and joie de vivre.

This is what I want to examine in the following sections of this book. Despite rather significant changes in the size, economy, and social and ethnic makeup of the region, the many and varied communities of the San Diego region have both retained their individual identities and ways of life and invented new ones. To a very real degree, local sense of place has been built around the topics I have discussed so far such as the perception of and attachment to the physical geography of the place, the utilization of a real or romanticized heritage in building for the future, and the creation of symbiotic economic relationships along the international border. The beaches, the mountains, the ranches, the Navy, the deserts, the architecture, and the climate all shape the ways in which ordinary San Diegans carry out their daily lives. San Diego has been designated an "All-American" city, but it is still unique in many ways. Much the same can be said about the neighborhoods that make up the metropolitan area. The purpose of this chapter has been to introduce a few "real" statistics about the people of San Diego and the ways they spend their days "getting and spending" in the region. The following chapters emphasize how this all plays out at the neighborhood level. Although I will use some data, the emphasis is on the more whimsical aspects of community character and sense of place. Even in the face of serious issues such as housing costs, ethnic diversity, and environmental hazards, many San Diego places have so far managed to maintain a quirky identity.

Lifestyle Zones in the Central City

To a very real degree, we see what we have words to describe. But many of our words, and thus our perceptions, are out of date. Many of our commonly used terms, such as central business district, inner city, and suburb, are no longer very useful in describing the sprawling, multi-centered metropolitan areas of today. In no urban area is this truer than in San Diego. In order to explore the various lifestyles in this region, therefore, I have chosen to describe examples of what I have called "lifestyle zones," that is, types of settings that display, illustrate, and even exude a particular relationship between people and their environment. They epitomize, in other words, the types of places that can result from attempts to conflate landscape and lifestyle. Beach towns dominated by surf shops and volleyball nets are an obvious type, but there are many more.

CLASSIC MODELS OF CITY STRUCTURE AND THE MODERN CITY

As academic writing on the city developed over the course of the twentieth century, scholars in several disciplines attempted to create convincing models of city structure and urban form. Whereas urban scholars in Europe often emphasized the roles

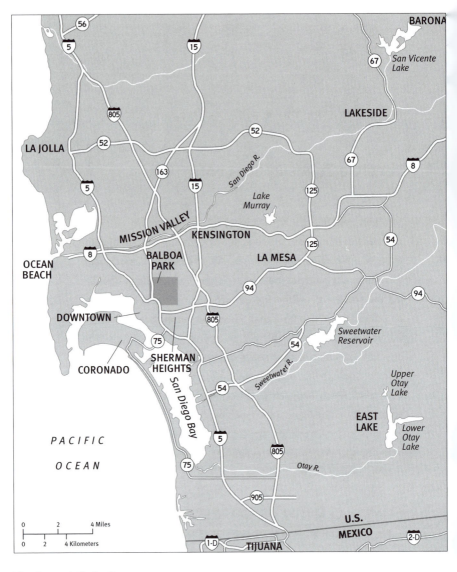

Lifestyle zones in the San Diego area.

of challenging physical sites, unique combinations of historical epochs, and local building materials and architectural preferences to "explain" the look and form of urban places, American writers most often used social and economic variables to illustrate patterns and processes. Using readily available data from the Census Bureau and similar agencies, modelers sought to explain city structure on the basis of socioeconomic variables such as land values, land uses, population density, housing quality, race and ethnicity, crime rates, and family stage. The task was simplified because zoning regulations caused American cities to be more segregated and predictable than those in most other parts of the world. Manufacturing, shopping, high density residential, recreation, and single-family houses had their own colors and locations on the zoning map. The three models that resulted from the use of these variables were the Concentric Zone Model, the Sector Model, and the Multiple Nuclei Model.[1]

The classic models, however, while they have had great heuristic value over the decades, leave out a great deal. There is little or no mention of topography, architectural traditions, landscape tastes, or social diversity unrelated to economic status or ethnicity. They have also had perhaps too much influence on the way we see and describe urban places. The Concentric Zone Model, for example, postulates a series of concentric rings with increasing status toward the outer rings. The inner rings include working-class tenements and skid rows; the outer ones have high status suburban characteristics. Partly as a result of this view of the city, we often use terms such as "inner city" or "suburban ring" in ways that make them synonymous with a socioeconomic category regardless of actual location. Poor, minority communities are often commonly referred to as inner city areas even when they are relatively rustic and remote, but high status areas never are, even if they are only blocks from the downtown core. Thus Roxbury and Watts are inner city but not Beacon Hill or Greenwich

Village. Similarly, the term suburban is normally interchangeable with higher status even though many edge-of-town locations are quite poor. The problems arise when the term are used as descriptors or even explanations for urban trends as in "that's an inner city problem."

The Sector and Multiple Nuclei Models have mitigated some of these perceptual problems, but they too have emphasized socioeconomic variables at the expense of more place-full attributes. Thus there are the sectoral "black belts" and "Gold Coasts" of Chicago, patterns that elucidate but also mask many local place characteristics.

A major criticism of the classic models is that they are quintessentially "modern" in that they assume a city structure built around the quest for economic efficiency, profit maximization, and social segregation. The modern city emphasized impersonal, mechanistic relationships and communities of interest rather than the totalizing communities of earlier cities. Thus concentric rings and sectors were seen as the natural result of the processes of sorting out people and activities in space based solely on the ability to pay for an accessible location. Relatively little attention was focused on the cultural meaning of these patterns and what it was like to experience day to day life in the modern city.

The modern city as an entity to be studied has been called into question by recent suggestions that we are now dealing with a "postmodern" world, a world of display, spectacle, pastiche, and whimsy.[2] The city is now divided into varying realms as much by different forms of consumption as by different levels of production, as developers must continuously create new market niches for those seeking to buy a lifestyle. The postmodern city emphasizes symbolism with heritage preservation, architectural references to the past, with the exotic, café-filled lifestyle zones, flexible sites of production, and ephemeral fashions largely replacing a simple division of the city into socioeconomic classes.

There may still be rings and sectors, but they are much richer and more complex than those of the classic models. These trends are gradually being incorporated into city planning regulations as the old "everything in its place" zoning laws are being rewritten to allow a variety of mixed-use projects and neighborhoods. A number of new ways to impose order on urban areas and to help us understand their increasing complexity have arisen over the past few decades that complement the modern/postmodern debate. I include a few of these approaches in the following paragraphs, but the case studies in this and later chapters will serve to expand the ideas.

NEW WAYS OF LOOKING AT METROPOLITAN REGIONS

Over the past few decades, a number of works have appeared that attempt to include aesthetic, physical, and perceptual factors in the creation of generalizations aimed at making sense of our vast metropolitan areas. Rayner Banham's 1971 *Los Angeles: The Architecture of Four Ecologies*, for example, demonstrates how the relationship between the physical setting and the built environment can be used to thicken our perception of urban places.[3] Banham suggests that the best way to understand Los Angeles, for example, is to examine its architecture in the context of four types of ecological zones. He dubs these zones Surfurbia, the Foothills, the Plains of Id, and Autopia. Each area has its own look and feel regardless of socioeconomic status or ethnicity. While not supplanting the more traditional procedures of urban analysis, Banham's scheme adds a delicious layer of colorful detail that helps make Los Angeles come alive as a real place. Malibu is very different from Pasadena despite similar incomes and housing values. Hollywood and Long Beach are very different, too.

While some of the characteristics of the classic ecological

models are evident in the San Diego region, patterns based on physical geography, such as those suggested by Banham, are equally important. Among these is a possible "Zonal Strip" model describing linear patterns of land use, socioeconomic characteristics, ethnic diversity, and even housing types inward from the coast to the mountains. The linear coastal zone, inland mesas, foothills, and mountains each have a predictable population profile in addition to a distinctive landscape personality. For example, the coastal zone has very little ethnic diversity since it is very heavily non-Hispanic white. The next zone is the most diverse with white, Hispanic, Asian, and African American pockets as well as many communities that are quite diverse. The "rustic suburb" foothill zone further inland is also predominantly white, but diversity increases even farther to the east with Native American reservations, retirement centers, and small mountain communities and border towns. On a map, ethnicity can thus be modeled, at least at a very general level, as a series of parallel north-south strips roughly corresponding to environmental characteristics and transportation corridors. This strip model also describes many variations in land use as well with the majority of "big footprint" buildings located in the inland mesa zone.

While it is both fun and occasionally informative to experiment with the classic ecological models and their many variations, understanding today's vast metropolitan areas requires a plethora of approaches. Over the years, of course, many new and different approaches have been used in the attempt to describe the tremendous internal variety of metropolitan areas. Many have emphasized place characteristics that are fuzzier and less data-driven than the ecological models. Walter Firey and others, for example, have emphasized how "sentiment and symbolism" can play important roles in location decisions and urban morphology quite apart from purely economic and social variables.[4] Firey, in describing such neighborhoods as Beacon Hill and the North End in Boston, argued that attachment to place should be considered at least as important as the ecological processes embedded in the classic "Chicago School" models. Historic neighborhoods, for example, can engender loyalty and a strong proprietary interest far beyond the actual economic value of local buildings.

Kevin Lynch reinforced the idea of place attachment with his work on the concept of urban imageability as discussed in the first chapter of this book.[5] People often become attached to highly legible districts and develop a proprietary attitude toward them. Thus the French Quarter in New Orleans and Greenwich Village in New York City are not simply old neighborhoods but places that loom large in the minds of the residents. If communities are legible, people can carry mental maps of them in their heads and are thus more likely to explore and linger in urban spaces. Lynch also explores the theme of planning and managing these sensory qualities of place at the regional scale.[6] He suggests that topics such as "esthetic and sensuous form" and "landscape as communication and symbol" should be better integrated with models of transportation and patterns of land use. As metropolitan regions expand to cover several thousand square miles, it is more important than ever to manage ways of helping people to become attached to the places they experience, even if they only move through them in automobiles.

Yi-Fu Tuan and Ted Relph have also explored the ways in which people attach themselves to places.[7] While these scholars, as well as many others, suggest that an abiding and authentic sense of place is more difficult to achieve than it was in days gone by, it is still a worthy goal that is possible to achieve. A key word here is "authenticity." As every city and neighborhood experiences increasing degrees of commodification and commercialization, the task of building genuine place-based communities has become problematic. Authentic "topophilia" or love of place is often replaced by developer hyperbole and tourist slogans. This is especially true in San Diego, a region that throughout its history has grown up with very large doses of real estate hype and tourism promotion.

The issue of authenticity involves a variety of dilemmas that cannot easily be resolved. Nevertheless, I will try to keep this reality in mind as I examine individual communities and lifestyles in the San Diego region. Neighborhoods usually do have an authentic sense of place, but, on the other hand, some try to milk their identity for all it is worth and so exaggerate their unique character and personality. As "culture" in American urban regions increasingly becomes a matter of picking and choosing locales and identities as much as an hereditary given, the variety of lifestyles in metropolitan regions has exploded. Reality is always a judicious mixture of fact and fantasy.

This mixture of fact and fantasy is especially important in the San Diego region. The combination of extreme variations in physical environment from beaches to mountains and deserts means that San Diegans can choose settings that reinforce even wildly romanticized lifestyles. Teachers and bankers can on the weekends be ranchers, foresters, surfers, and prospectors. Historical legends focusing on Native Americans, Spaniards, miners, and the Navy also provide grist for the lifestyle mill. In addition, topographical separation often makes it easier to define and "protect" place-based communities and keep them from becoming engulfed in an endless, homogeneous sprawl.

Real estate agents build on the idea of exaggerated place identity and attempt to steer potential buyers into the realm of their dreams. According to research by geographer Brenda Kayzar, advertisements for housing in the San Diego region, for example, often depict lifestyle zones and overall setting as much or more than detailed housing characteristics.[8] Ads for houses in the suburb of La Mesa, for example, emphasize the value of living in a place with that "friendly, small town feel," while those for

Fallbrook push the theme of picturesque rusticity and rural ambience. Advertisements are as likely to show scenes of parades, vineyards, forests, mountain views, or beaches as actual houses. Ads for houses in and around downtown San Diego speak vividly of access to theaters, opera, museums, and fine dining, and show pictures of people in formal attire descending a loft stairway holding glasses of wine and bouquets of flowers. The details of the actual houses sometimes come only as an afterthought. These ads demonstrate extreme variations even when holding housing and rent values even. There is nearly as much variety within every income group than there is between them.

Several authors have attempted to get at some of these variations through the analysis of magazine subscriptions and other indicators of social class and taste. Maps of ZIP codes, as suggested by Michael Weiss in *The Clustering of America*, can be analyzed to show groupings of Volvo-driving young professionals and blue-collar low riders.[9] This information is obviously related to the theme of placemaking that I am chasing, but I am going at it from a slightly different angle. As people search for an ecological niche to build their lives around, they also endeavor to reshape the landscape and enhance its imagery. People, in other words, attempt to do for neighborhoods what Ramona did for the image of San Diego as a whole. If the setting is rustic, businesses specializing in barns and picket fences thrive. If a small town image is sought, residents quickly begin planning holiday parades and window decorations. Although they may have many of the same concerns—traffic, safety, schools, property values, and the like—a lot of people want to live in a place that is different. In San Diego, it is relatively easy to satisfy this want.

As I explore life in the San Diego Metropolitan Region in the next three chapters, I build on these and other basic ideas. I begin with a group of older neighborhoods in the central zones of the urban area and discuss both their commonalities a la the classic models of city structure and their unique identities as imageable places. In the following two chapters, I work outward to suburban and exurban locales following the same modus operandi. I call the neighborhoods I examine "epitome places" in that I use them to epitomize a certain type of community and resident. Every urban region contains such epitome places, but San Diego, with its beaches, mountains, border towns, and reservations, has far more than most metropolitan areas of its size.

OCEAN BEACH AS A PLACE OF RESISTANCE

Since San Diego is known throughout the country as a beach town, or more accurately a series of beach towns, each with its own personality, Ocean Beach is a good place to start the San Diego story. Ocean Beach is a place of resistance: resistance to the forces of social and cultural homogenization and resistance to the physical forces of beach erosion. It is thus a good example of a community that is attempting to "hang on" in the face of sometimes overwhelming odds. Ocean Beach also exudes a powerful sense of community. "Obeacians," as many residents call themselves, have "I love OB" stickers on their cars and bikes and take great pride in being part of what they see to be an unusual place. At one time a radio show featured the ongoing exploits of the "OB Ranger," and OB T-shirts with crazy slogans and symbols abound. Some would say that OB is caught in a 1960s time warp or at least wants to be. Others see it as an undervalued piece of real estate just ripe for investment and hyperdevelopment. The reality is probably somewhere in between.

Ocean Beach was the closest ocean front community to both downtown and Old Town San Diego, at least for those not wishing to take a ferry to Coronado. It began in the boom of the 1880s with high aspirations. During the peak of the land speculation furor in 1887, Frank Higgins and William Carlson purchased 600 acres of land in a place called Mussel Beds. Intending to create a classic seasonal oceanfront community, they changed the name to Ocean Beach and filled the plat map with street names that referenced beach resorts all over the world, such as Newport, Santa Cruz, Niagara, and Brighton. In April, Higgins and Carlson flooded San Diego with promotional materials urging people to "build a cottage by the sea," following up with a free mussel roast that attracted over one thousand people to the barren site. An estimated 2,500 lots were sold (at $60.00 each) on the first day, and prices rose to over $300.00 by the end of the summer. Promoters became more and more ecstatic and began to compare Ocean Beach with the Garden of Eden and other paradisiacal locales.[10]

In 1888, the Cliff House Hotel, the area's first significant commercial destination, was built. It was a miniature version of the Hotel del Coronado, complete with a ballroom for special events. Also as in Coronado, a rail line was built from the Bay to Ocean Beach so people could travel there from downtown by ferry and train if they did not want to make the "long" journey by coach. Unlike Coronado, however, the success of Ocean Beach as a major seasonal and tourist destination was short-lived. The real estate boom collapsed in late 1888 and the hotel burned down in 1898. Ten years later there were still only eighteen houses in the area, most of them shacks. OB's first era had come to an end and there was little to show for it. Picnics were the main activity. The stage was unwittingly set for the "second string," somewhat marginalized and Bohemian image that OB would retain into the future.

The second era began in about 1910. A new generation of promoters saw to it that the community had utilities, graded streets, and rail connections, and a new round of development and speculation was underway. Stores, restaurants, and a boardwalk appeared and OB was advertised as a "pretty" place with all the modern conveniences. There were more than 100 houses and the beginnings of a neighborhood atmosphere. The keystone in the latest attempt to put the area on the map, however, was Wonderland, a large seaside amusement park. The grand opening was July 4, 1913, and it was reported that 35,000 people came to celebrate the event, a remarkable (and perhaps exaggerated) number given that there were only 62,000 people in the county. Wonderland had forty attractions, including the largest roller coaster on the West Coast, water slide, skating rink, carousel, and zoo. There were also a pier, bathhouses, and food stands. A promotional brochure praised the creation of Wonderland and stated that it "completely assures the future of this place as a popular resort." But it was not to be. Wonderland lasted for only two seasons, and its demise illustrates the importance of both social and physical forces in shaping Ocean Beach. The opening of the Panama-California Exposition in Balboa Park in 1915–16 drew crowds away from the amusement park. In the winter of 1916, high surf washed sand from under the roller coaster and it was never repaired. The park never reopened, and Ocean Beach failed again in its bid to be a major destination in Southern California. Still, for a while it looked like the community would recover at least some of its resort personality. A saltwater plunge was opened in 1916 and a merry-go-round in 1918. A new resort hotel opened in 1919 and summer crowds were festive.

Competition emerged in 1925, however, when a new amusement park opened in nearby and newly accessible Mission Beach. The new park had a giant roller coaster, the largest indoor pool in America, a dance hall with a permanent orchestra, and modern electric streetcar service to both central San Diego and La Jolla. The Ocean Beach carousel closed in 1927, and there were no more attempts to create a notable resort. Ocean Beach gradually became a neighborhood that just happened to be by the sea. By

1928 there were approximately 6,000 residents and 40 stores and restaurants. Flimsy beach cottages were joined by more substantial houses as the community took on a kind of small town atmosphere. Still, there were more vacant lots than anything else. Like most of America, Ocean Beach grew slowly during the depression years of the 1930s. By 1940, the gradual growth over the past half-century had created a diverse landscape of beach cottages, substantial houses from a variety of architectural eras, and many types of business establishments from hotels to garages. Another boom, however, was on the horizon, and it came during the war years of the 1940s.

Consolidated Aircraft Corporation, which was located very close to Ocean Beach along the streetcar line toward downtown San Diego, was called upon to build thousands of airplanes for Great Britain as early as 1941. Consolidated doubled its number of employees, and many lived in the greater Point Loma-Ocean Beach area. When the U.S. became a combatant, the federal government gave San Diego fifteen million dollars to construct housing to accommodate population growth. Military facilities were expanded along San Diego Bay only a few miles from Ocean Beach. OB was now a Navy town. In some ways, the character of the community changed again. Rentals were in great demand. Cafes did a good business and their numbers increased dramatically. Sailors added a certain personality to the beachfront ambience.

Between 1940 and 1950, about 1,600 single-family homes were built in Ocean Beach, over 40 percent of the total housing stock. The community of 10,000 also became increasingly differentiated between the older, quintessentially "beachy" areas to the north and the more suburban neighborhoods to the south and east.[11]

The boom continued during the Korean War, but its architectural impact changed. For the first time, a substantial number of apartment buildings were put up, since the vacant lots of earlier eras had disappeared. By 1960, over 800 units had been built in structures with at least five units. More than one-third of all Obeacians were now apartment dwellers, especially along the water in the older, former resort district. The combination of modest apartment buildings and older beach cottages made Ocean Beach one of the cheapest beach communities in the region. The average price for a house was actually well below the city average in 1960, and rents were barely above the average despite the summer influx of tourists. Many people were concerned about what was viewed as serious deterioration and blight. Newspaper articles appeared in the late 1950s deploring the prevalence of prostitution and narcotics in the area, and discussions of possible redevelopment strategies began. Much of Ocean Beach was old, underplanned, and poorly built. In some ways it fit the definition of a seaside "inner city." The automobile had made a long string of beaches farther north easily accessible and access by public transit was becoming a mixed blessing.

In 1958, the Citizens' Ocean Beach Improvement Committee with the Urban Renewal Commission and the City Planning Commission drafted a redevelopment plan for the community aimed at improving the "blighted, antiquated business and residential area." The plan covered 32 acres and called for large hotels and motels fronting a new pedestrian mall. There was a public outcry and the plan was defeated, the first example of what would become a long history of organized resistance to change in OB. No sooner was the threat withdrawn than a new plan appeared in 1960 that would have turned the beach into a state park with a fence, a large parking lot, and admission charges. It too was defeated. In 1970, plans to extend a protective jetty at the northern end of OB were announced, largely for the purpose of flood control along the San Diego River. Hundreds of protesters gathered to stop the project, arguing that it was the first step toward massive redevelopment projects aimed at tourists rather than locals. The jetty was stopped at the high tide mark. Resistance to change and outsiders was becoming a community theme.

Despite antidevelopment sentiment, over 1,100 apartment units were put up during the 1960s and by 1970, 76 percent of OB's housing was renter occupied. Average incomes, rents, and housing values were all low, and the area became known as a center for counter-culture and resistance. By the late 1960s, the area was increasingly associated with "hippies," and many feared that it would become a seaside Haight-Ashbury. Young people flocked to the area. Its complex and multi-layered image had largely taken shape but there was one missing element: the rich.

Battles over community plans and redevelopment schemes continued into the 1970s, but housing values had begun their inexorable rise in all of California, especially along the coast. The community's diversity once again increased as well-heeled professionals moved into the fringes of the old beach town. The core of the old resort with its flimsy cottages and cheap apartments became known as the "Combat Zone" and exuded a colorful counter-culture, but the houses uphill were attracting people with money who wanted unobstructed views of the ocean. A new alliance gradually took shape that joined all those opposed to high-rise tourist developments like those that had recently appeared in places like La Jolla. OB's reputation for lively and sometimes illegal nonconformity was useful in thwarting large, upscale projects.

Ocean Beach Today

Ocean Beach is getting smaller, but today the threat comes from the expanding high-income neighborhoods nearby rather than destructive waves. At most, three small census tracts containing

Ocean Beach, a landscape of resistance to both physical and social change.

a population of about 12,000 define the community, but even this exaggerates its size since only the core area exhibits many classic OB characteristics. Maintaining the personality of Ocean Beach depends in part on preserving its built environment, but unlike many historic districts, most of OB's architectural heritage is of marginal value. The tiny and often shoddily constructed beach cottages on postage stamp lots that make up much of the OB core are sitting on very valuable land these days. But since they are difficult to upgrade and lot assembly can be tricky, many of them remain. Property owners may view them as long-term investments that can bring in rental income with a minimum of maintenance. The boxy 1950s-era apartment buildings interspersed with the cottages are also without much architectural merit, but they serve a purpose. Without this type of housing, Ocean Beach would be-come just another upscale beach town.

A preservation ethic of sorts also prevails in the commercial "downtown" of Ocean Beach. The buildings on Newport Avenue, the "main drag," have changed occupants many times but few have been substantially upgraded. Newport is an officially designated "Antiques" district and many of the old grocery and hardware stores now contain old furniture and sundry arts and crafts. This is somewhat ironic given that OB has a median age of about thirty and its local ambience depends on a transient, early twenties "surfer culture" to keep it viable. Antiques are probably not a high priority. The stores bring money into the community, however, and help to keep the business district alive. OB has done its best to keep out chain stores and restaurants and consequently has a large number of strange and funky cafes and bars. "Head shops" such as the Black seem left over from the 1960s, as do many of the people on the streets nearby. Some stores have been decorated with colorful murals and hand-painted signage. Surfboards, headbands, and sweet-perfumed antiwar rallies continue to add character to the place in the shadow of hillside homes selling for a minimum of $750,000. Despite the plentiful "No Starbucks in OB" signs, there is one now, albeit a rather heavily fortified version. It is surrounded, however, by homegrown businesses such as the Endless Summer Drive-Through Espresso Stand.

Ocean Beach is a kind of mine canary for the existence of a diversity of lifestyles in the San Diego coastal strip. If it can hold out in the face of tremendous speculative pressures then there is still hope for authentic place making on the beach. If it succumbs to development and homogenization, it will be just another location for upscale condos and seaside resorts. For now, however, a relatively wide range of incomes and lifestyles persists, with even the rich folks on the hill reveling in the offbeat personality of the place.

SAN DIEGO ''SPANISH'' IN SHERMAN HEIGHTS AND KENSINGTON

Sherman Heights and Kensington are both older residential communities, but they illustrate several different trends or "fates" in the making of the San Diego sense of place. Sherman Heights is largely Latino and has been for several decades, while Kensington is one of the most heavily Anglo neighborhoods in central San Diego. The two neighborhoods epitomize the irony mentioned in Chapter 1 in that Latino Sherman Heights contains mostly Victorian and Craftsman cottages complete with white picket fences while Anglo Kensington exudes a Spanish/Mediterranean architectural flavor. Today the neighborhoods represent two completely different ways of creating and maintaining what might be called "Hispanic landscape tastes."

Kensington, developed mostly during the 1920s and 1930s, has maintained and expanded its red-tiled Spanish architecture while adding an increasing amount of xerophytic Mediterranean vegetation. It is well known for its picturesque character and sense of place. For many, it represents the way San Diego should look. Sherman Heights, on the other hand, is Hispanic in population but not architecture. It was built largely during the late 1800s with Italianate, Queen Anne, Romanesque, Craftsman, and neo-Classical architecture predominating. It is now an officially designated Historic District but there is little consensus about how the neighborhood should look. Many of the residents have been busy creating their own version of a Spanish landscape—one that is often at odds with the official architectural guidelines.

Sherman Heights

Sherman Heights is one of the oldest neighborhoods in San Diego. Originally part of a vaguely defined community just uphill from the eastern edge of downtown known as Golden Hill, the distinctive neighborhood of Sherman Heights was first laid out by Matthew Sherman in the late 1860s. Since the area was considered to be an ideal suburban location with easy access to the city and the waterfront, a variety of pleasant Victorian single-family houses were built from the 1870s to the crash of 1893. When construction resumed in the early 1900s, craftsman bungalows were all the rage. Both mansions and cottages are common on the uniform, grid-pattern streets. By the 1880s, streetcar lines helped the greater Golden Hill area, including Sherman Heights, to become a premier residential address. Residents included three mayors, two state senators, a city councilman, a Superior Court judge, and several business leaders. In 1887, the latter group even constructed one of the most elaborate and exotic mansions in San Diego, now known as the Villa Montezuma, in the hope of persuading Jesse Shephard, a leading opera singer, to remain in the city and contribute to its culture. The plan failed, but the house remains an important historic site.

As the twentieth century unfolded, competition increased for the title of ideal suburban retreat. The primary threats to the prominence of Golden Hill were the neighborhoods north of downtown along the west side of Balboa Park. Variously known as Uptown, West Park, and Hillcrest, these neighborhoods had better access to the cultural facilities in the park's Prado area and benefited from the Panama-California Exposition in 1915. The area was in the primary "zone of assimilation" for the expanding downtown, and several large apartment buildings, hotels, and medical complexes emerged there by the 1920s. Golden Hill was being left behind. As automobiles made even remote locations such as La Jolla accessible, competition increased dramatically.

The Golden Hill region was also too close to the gradually industrializing waterfront. As a result, the community became increasingly differentiated between the desirable north, along the southern edge of Balboa Park, and the disheveled south, with its warehouses, boatyards, and sheds. The community began to suffer during the depression years and the war years that followed. Many of the large Victorian houses were subdivided into tenements and the percentage of rentals skyrocketed. This happened at a time when most of the houses were in need of major upgrades in plumbing, heating, electricity, roofing, and general infrastructure. Victorian architecture was also considered to be passé if not downright ugly by the mid-twentieth century, and it was common for such houses to be portrayed as haunted, or at the very least filled with stray cats and weird characters (think of *Psycho* or the Addams Family). By the 1950s, many Sherman Heights houses were in sad shape.

A major disruption occurred during the late 1950s when a freeway (state highway 94) was built through the heart of the community. Population plummeted as hundreds of houses were removed and the noise and dirt of construction further diminished any claims to high status. By the time the highway opened in 1960, the area was well on its way to being a low-income, heavily minority neighborhood. The freeway also created a clear consensus boundary between the northern and southern parts of the community. A few years later, a second freeway (Interstate 5) separated the residential communities from the downtown core to the west.

As the greater Golden Hill area was carved up by highways and varying social trends and policies, it became increasingly differentiated. After considerable dead-end tries, four neighborhoods were eventually identified and named: Golden Hill, Sherman Heights, Grant Hill (named after Ulysses Grant, Jr. an early developer), and Logan Heights (later Barrio Logan). Golden Hill, adjacent to Balboa Park, benefited from its separate identity and began to experience some renovation and gentrification in the 1960s and 1970s while the other three became increasingly poor and Latino. With the exception of the northern fringe, the communities all experienced a high degree of redlining by banks and savings institutions with many census tracts having no mortgage loans as late as 1975.[12] Anti-redlining laws have had some impact but, with many structures in disrepair, loans can still be problematic. This is especially true in Barrio Logan, where junk-yards and warehouses are interspersed with housing.

In the middle of the north to south social gradient is Sherman Heights. Sherman Heights occupies approximately fifty blocks with about forty blocks included in the Sherman Heights Historic District. Established in 1987, eight years after the Golden Hill Historic District, the official designation was aimed at stopping the demolition of valued architecture and the insertion of nonconforming building types and land uses. A survey at that time determined that 76 percent of the structures were historically important. Prior to the mid-1980s when an emergency moratorium ordinance on the issuance of demolition and removal permits was put in place, the district was subject only to citywide zoning laws. The result was the insertion of a large number of high-density nonconforming structures. Perhaps the last straw for preservationists occurred when a magnificent Victorian mansion was rolled down the hill and shipped across the bay to Coronado. The architectural treasures of Sherman Heights were literally being moved away for renovation in "better" neighborhoods. Preservation policies in Sherman Heights have been only partly successful in stopping change, however, although the changes have become less drastic and more reversible in recent years.

Much of the problem stems from the fact that the preservationists have very different landscape tastes. Quite apart from the high costs involved in accurate restorations, the two groups simply have very different idealized images of what the community should look like. One is Anglo-Victorian while the other is Modern-Mexican. The Sherman Heights-Grant Hill neighborhood (hereafter referred to as Sherman Heights) is about 90 percent Latino, well past the threshold for the creation of a uniformly ethnic cultural community. The total population for the two census tracts is 7,352 people, up from 5,900 in 1980. Most of this increase is due to larger households, since few new dwelling units have been added in recent years. In fact, the population is roughly what it was in 1950 despite subsequent losses in housing due to freeway construction. The average household in Sherman Heights consists of just under four people, almost double the average for the city of San Diego and the somewhat gentrified district of nearby Golden Hill. Children and extended family activities make up a significant part of what can be classified as the community landscape. The median age is about twenty-four, nearly ten years lower than California as a whole.

Sherman Heights was built before Southern California became Spanish. Its Carpenter Gothic and Craftsman houses and tree-lined streets could easily be in Georgia or Oregon. Geographer Daniel Arreola, writing about urban landscapes in Arizona and Texas, has suggested that when a neighborhood becomes overwhelmingly Hispanic (75–80 percent), its landscape begins to change dramatically.[13] The five major components of this change are house color, fencing and fence types, murals, vegetation, and yard shrines. In addition, the language of the signs becomes Latino on commercial buildings and churches. Ethnic personalization takes place regardless of the original size and style of the architecture. Despite its designation as a historic district and its proximity to considerable gentrification in downtown San Diego and Golden Hill, Sherman Heights is becoming increasingly Hispanic or Latino in appearance. According to a detailed study of the neighborhood by geographer/planner Robert Rundle, all five of the landscape features identified by Arreola are evident.[14] Most of the changes have occurred over the past two decades as the "Mexicaness" of the community has settled in. In the process of becoming Latino, both white and black populations have been displaced and ethnic diversity has diminished.

Perhaps the most notable Latino landscape feature in Sherman Heights is fenced front yards. While Anglo neighborhoods tend to favor (and in some cases mandate) open, grass lawns, the Latino tradition emphasizes an enclosed courtyard in front of houses. This is increasingly evident in Sherman Heights, where nearly two-thirds of the lots display front yard fences. The percentage would be higher except that fences rarely appear in front of apartment buildings and commercial establishments. The predominant material used for fencing is chain link, but this is a function more of low incomes and renter occupancy than of landscape tastes. In many cases, extremely ornate and substantial fencing appears when the occupants decide to make a commitment to the residence. Fences of stone, brick, wood, concrete block, and wrought iron are common and these and other materials are sometimes used in elaborate combinations.

Still, much of the fencing used to create enclosed spaces does not conform to the overall architectural ambience. In conjunction with its preservation ordinances, the city has classified fences as either traditional or nontraditional. Traditional fences are those that match or at least complement the architecture of the house. In a neighborhood where Victorian and Craftsman homes predominate, the options for traditional fencing are few and include such styles as white picket and certain types of stone. Where Mediterranean architecture is present, stucco and wrought iron fencing is acceptable. These kinds of fences are expensive to construct and are most likely to be built by homeowners rather than renters. As a result, about 82 percent of the 600-plus front yard fences in Sherman Heights are classified as nonconforming.

Most of these fences do not conform to either San Diego's general residential zoning regulations or the guidelines in the historic district designation. Since they are a highly valued and maybe even a culturally required landscape element, however, getting rid of them would not be an easy task. The neighborhood likes not only fences but also the kinds of enclosed spaces they help create.

Latino front yards tend to be very different from those in Anglo

Hispanic landscapes in Sherman Heights—Victorian houses, fences, vegetation, and additions.

neighborhoods. While most Americans prefer an open, grass lawn in the English tradition, Latino yards are more likely to have flowers, vegetables, potted plants, and occasional religious shrines. Toys and even playground equipment are also more common. In part, this is because front yards are more likely to be thought of as usable areas rather than simple open spaces. Large families and the need for flexible play space along with rental status may encourage the use of movable potted plants over permanent landscaping. While not common, religious shrines, often built in response to a crisis, are also perceived as a perfectly acceptable use for a front yard.

The use of vivid color is also a widespread characteristic in many heavily Latino communities. Ironically, Victorian houses often featured a plethora of strong colors with contrasting trim when they were first built, but over the years they were generally subdued as middle-class American values came to favor whites and beiges. Today, many neighborhoods in San Diego have codes and covenants that require that all houses be off-white or beige, and people defend these regulations by saying that they live in fear of someone painting a home green or purple. In Sherman Heights, however, things have come full circle and bright colors are making a comeback.

About 20 percent, or about 200, of the houses in Sherman Heights exhibit what might be called "bright" paint colors. The approximate percentage is necessary since there is no consensus definition of what constitutes a Latino color. In addition, sometimes bright pastel colors are used for an entire structure, while in other cases only the trim is painted in an unusual hue. Bright colors are relatively uncommon for large apartment buildings in Sherman Heights, but they are also more frequently used for such structures throughout the city than for single-family homes. It is therefore harder to classify such buildings as Latino. The situation is also complicated by the fact that gentrification often involves the reintroduction of interesting color schemes, especially for Victorian houses. Sherman Heights is a colorful place for a variety of reasons. Wall murals, especially on commercial structures, and colorful signage add to the character of the community.

The personalization of place through the use of color and Latino murals is well illustrated by Chicano Park, in the neighborhood now called Barrio Logan just south of Sherman Heights.[15] The park represents perhaps the first and certainly the best publicized example of the battle for "ethnic ownership" of a landscape in San Diego. The Coronado Bridge linking Coronado to San Diego was completed in 1969. The massive entry ramp was built in the marginal semi-industrial neighborhood then known as Logan Heights, and plans were made to build a State Highway Patrol center in the cleared space under the bridge along with a tiny 1.6-acre park. The symbolism of the plan was not lost on the community. In 1971, more than 1,000 people gathered in the park to protest. Soon colorful murals depicting various aspects of the Mexican-American experience in California began to appear on

Chicano Park: Hispanic murals on the Coronado Bridge near Sherman Heights.

the bridge stanchions. Rallies were held to oppose the Highway Patrol office and to set the area aside for a much larger (eight-acre) community park. The state relented and worked out a land swap so that the entire area could be a park. The park buildings were to be built in a red-tiled Spanish style. Again the neighborhood objected. The people wanted the central kiosk to be in Aztec style, a style that was meant to predate and even repudiate the pervasive romantic Spanish character of San Diego. As the park evolved, professional artists were brought in from around the state to create murals on the bridge supports.

In March 1980, the Historical Site Board of the City of San Diego designated Chicano Park a historical site. The murals, it was argued, accurately and symbolically depicted the life experiences of Latinos in California and so were authentically historic. And so it was that official historic designation and Latino landscape tastes were conflated. The stage was set for Latino personalization of Sherman Heights, and indeed the entire greater Golden Hill community.

Kensington

The Kensington-Talmadge area of San Diego exudes a very different kind of Latino landscape. Kensington-Talmadge (hereafter simply Kensington) was one of San Diego's first quintessentially suburban areas. Kensington Park, the first development, was officially opened in 1910 in a rural area well beyond the city limits but at the end of a new trolley line. It is widely regarded, at least locally, as one of the first planned suburbs with its numerous restrictions on land use and design. Examples include statements that "each residence shall cost not less than $2,000" and "no part of said building shall be located nearer than twenty feet to the front of said lot." In addition, no fences of any kind were to be allowed in front of the houses. These restrictions remained in place only until 1926, but an architectural review board continued until 1948.[16] Symbolic gates marked the entrance to the neighborhood, and sidewalks and street lighting were of the highest quality. No commercial activities were permitted in the community.

There were also racial covenants of a type that were common in San Diego between 1910 and the late 1940s when they were declared "unenforceable" by the U.S. Supreme Court. No lot or house could be conveyed to anyone who was not of the "white or Caucasian race."

The first houses built in Kensington Park were wooden shingle-style California bungalows, and most were within a few blocks of the streetcar line. Since the area was laid out by a group of financiers led by an Anglophile Canadian, G. Aubrey Davidson, both the subdivision name and most of the street names paid homage to London. Very few houses were built in the English Tudor style, however. Enthusiasm for the new "Spanish" architecture inspired by the Panama-California Exhibition in 1915–16 was just beginning to take hold when construction came to a halt in World War I.

When construction resumed in the prosperous 1920s, Kensington became the most uniformly Spanish neighborhood in the San Diego region. Indeed, "Kensington Spanish" became a widely used descriptor for certain San Diego housing styles. New subdivisions like Kensington Heights and Kensington Manor were grafted onto the original community and featured picturesque, winding streets and the first underground electrical lines in the city. The combination of strict codes, new automobile accessibility, and exotic architecture made Kensington one of the most desirable residential communities in the city.

One reason for its desirability was its location on a mesa surrounded by a series of finger canyons on three sides. It was thus close to yet protected from the perceived chaos of the still unzoned city. Canyons also provided marvelous views and a sense of openness for those who lived at the edge. From the mid-1920s on, palatial houses with decks and swimming pools appeared in increasing numbers. On the southern margins of the community where there were no canyons, a mismatched street grid kept people from speeding into the neighborhood.

When the original controls ended in 1926, some of the older houses along the Adams Avenue streetcar line were replaced by commercial structures, including stores and a movie theater. Schools, churches, and a library appeared, and the community became even more self-contained. Throughout the 1920s and 1930s, however, the Spanish personality of the neighborhood was maintained and even enhanced as red tile and white stucco filled the mesa top. Local architect Richard Requa visited Spain (financed by the Portland Cement Company, a maker of stucco) and took extensive photographs of "typical Andalusian villages" for inclusion in popular literature promoting the new "ideal California dwellings." The original rather boxy style was gradually embellished with rounded towers, archways, wrought iron, and a variety of "authentic" plantings. Building came to a halt and housing values plummeted during the early 1930s as the Great Depression set in, but the community began to grow once again by 1936. Highly ornate Spanish architecture gradually lost favor and by the 1940s, it was largely seen as too expensive and simpler styles prevailed. By then, however, the look of Kensington had been established.

By the late 1930s, the community was rapidly outgrowing its infrastructure capacity. Water had always been a problem, and the residents also paid more for gas, trash collection, (private) police protection, and electricity than did residents of nearby communities. Without a good water supply, residents of Kensington also paid higher insurance rates. By 1936, most of Kensington had agreed to be annexed to the city of San Diego. Only Kensington Park, the original development, held out until 1953. Taxes doubled but services increased dramatically as the area became part of the city. Its design was quintessentially suburban but it was well connected by transportation systems and public services to the city. By the late 1940s, Kensington had become one of the most expensive residential areas in San Diego. Even today, it is seen as a quiet and highly desirable retreat conveniently located in the middle of the sprawling metropolitan area.

If anything, the landscape has become even more "Spanish" in recent years as new residents have upgraded older homes and added a variety of Mediterranean features such as patios, archways, towers, and second story balconies. Many front yards have changed as well. As water has once again become a serious problem in San Diego, many residents have moved away from the green lawn to types of vegetation that require less water. This is especially true in upscale neighborhoods where people can afford to hire gardeners who specialize in the new, conservation-oriented look. The trend has served to enhance the "Spanishness" of Kensington since desert vegetation, wildflowers, and tiled patios filled with succulents and flowers in colorful Mexican pots add to the community's exotic ambience. Low stucco walls covered with bougainvillea and punctuated by an occasional giant yucca have enclosed many front yards. One can almost hear the guitars and taste the tequila. There remains, however, a big difference between the look of the houses and the look of the people. Census tract 20.01, which includes most of Kensington, counted 3,328 people in the year 2000, more than 3,000 of them non-Hispanic whites. Latinos made up about 7 percent of the population. The adjacent Talmadge tract was similar, with about 8 percent. The percentage of Latinos was higher in South Kensington, though this is difficult to determine due to overlapping and fuzzy neighborhood boundaries. But even there, only about 15 percent of the population is Hispanic, compared to over 60 percent in tracts just south of the greater Kensington area. Kensington's population is also relatively older, with an average age of forty-seven in the central tract. Some young families may be dissuaded from living here by the high minority percentages in the public schools. But with house prices starting at about $500,000, it is not really a starter community for young families.

The exotic landscape is misleading. As the population becomes more Latino to the south of Kensington, the prevalence of formal Spanish architecture diminishes. As we have seen in Sherman Heights, however, informal Latino landscape characteristics often increase in number even in the absence of red tile. The landscapes of residential areas in central San Diego are far more interesting to examine than those in most of the newer developments since the controls are likely to be informal and reflect consensus community values rather than the official codes and restrictions found in planned unit projects. These are the neighborhoods that are continuously inventing and reinventing San Diego's identity. To a very real degree, San Diegans seek neigh-

Spanish architecture such as this in Kensington is usually associated with a non-Hispanic population.

borhoods where their cultural values and identity can be on display.

THE CREATION OF URBANITY IN DOWNTOWN SAN DIEGO

With a population of about 24,000 people in 2002, downtown San Diego has become one of the city's largest and fastest growing residential areas. New apartment and condominium towers are going up everywhere and there are plans to increase the population to 50,000 by the year 2020.[17] Nearly all the new housing and most of the new residents are in the luxury or at least upper-middle-class category, and this is an entirely new phenomenon in the region. As recently as the 1970s, there were virtually no up-scale residences downtown and very few could be counted as even middle class. Downtown as a residential community has been completely transformed. It is a perfect example for the theme of invention of lifestyles and landscapes in the San Diego region. The creation of a new downtown has taken a great deal of effort and the images and role models have, for the most part, not been local.

The cranes are still up and the construction dust has not settled, so it is too soon to analyze in any detail just who will live in the various downtown neighborhoods. Most of the larger projects were started after the 2000 census, and many of the buildings that were completed by then have only recently been converted to condominiums or otherwise modified in some way. The only thing that is certain is that today there are lots of expensive housing units in downtown San Diego and lots more on the way. By late 2002, there were sixty residential projects approved or under construction in downtown San Diego, with a target of an additional 8,200 new residential units by 2006. Whether these units will turn out to be part of viable neighborhoods or simply places for wealthy investors to dump money until more lucrative options come along remains to be seen. For now, it appears that the former, more optimistic view will prevail.

Downtown and Urban Decline

One of the most pervasive myths in the study of American cities is that downtowns were once important residential neighborhoods and that efforts should be made to bring people *back* downtown. In reality, the American central business district or CBD has, by definition, never been residential and the idea of having a large downtown residential population has emerged relatively recently.

Part of the problem has to do with the changing definition of downtown and part with the changing definition of residential population. Today, for example, downtown San Diego consists of over 1,400 acres or just over two square miles. The "official" downtown is defined by an inner belt freeway loop that separates

San Diego Bay and downtown San Diego from the air.

the largely commercial core from the neighborhoods beyond. But the area is far larger than the actual central business district, and therein lies much of the confusion. While San Diego had 20,333 people living in what is now defined as "downtown" in 1950, most of them lived in the 1,287 single-family houses on the margins of the area and did not consider themselves to be downtown at all. Average incomes approached the city median and households often consisted of families of three or four people.

Before the combination of commercial encroachment, especially gas stations, motels, and drive-in restaurants, and enclosure by the freeway during the 1950s, people in these zones usually identified with neighborhoods beyond the fuzzy downtown boundary.[18] As these houses were cleared for highways and commercial uses, the population plummeted. By 1970, there were only 562 single-family houses downtown, nearly all in "remnant neighborhoods" and in poor condition. They were awaiting demolition for higher and better uses, or at least parking lots, and so little or no investment for repair or even minimal maintenance occurred. Downtown was not a place for houses and grass lawns, and all the downtown census tracts were in the low-income category. Only 8,648 mostly single people still lived downtown. The problem was that there was simply no place for middle- or even low-income families to live downtown in 1970. There were only three options: run-down remnant houses, single-room occupancy hotels, and a few (often church-built) retirement complexes. Downtown people were old and poor and usually lived alone. Much of the population loss between 1950 and 1970 was due to smaller household size. People who could get out of downtown usually did so.

Downtown was generally moribund in 1970. Despite the construction of a half-dozen modest office towers, most activities were leaving. The single small downtown department store closed in the early 1970s and Navy-oriented clothing shops and tattoo parlors dominated the retailing that remained. The major convention facility was located in Mission Valley, and conference hotels were more common there and on Harbor Island than downtown. The downtown waterfront was lined with storage facilities and junkyards, and so few people saw the bay as a downtown amenity.

Reinventing Downtown

According to the classic models of city structure, American downtowns typically consist of a nonresidential central business district or CBD surrounded by a run-down transition zone, often referred to as skid row. In this generalization, there is a high-density core of office buildings, department stores, and hotels surrounded by a lower density frame of parking lots, sleazy bars, pool parlors, and remnant warehouses. The frame was called the transition zone because it was thought to be "in transition" as the downtown expanded outward and gradually took over the marginal spaces nearby. The expected transition, however, never arrived in most downtowns. The combination of high-rise con-struction, which concentrated CBD activities into a few blocks, and the appeal of increasingly attractive suburban options meant that the frame remained nearly empty for decades. Most down-towns came to have a negative image since it was necessary to pass through the disheveled frame in order to get to the gleaming core. With the slowdown in downtown office construction during the 1990s, it became evident that the office core would not be taking over the adjacent frame or transition zone any time in the foreseeable future. Something else was needed if downtowns were going to be successful.

In order to revitalize the frame, it had to be divided into several distinctive subdistricts, each with its own character, identity, land uses, and, perhaps most important, a name. Big footprint build-ings such as convention centers and sports arenas were used not only to soak up excess space but also to provide a theme for a sub-district. In this way, the downtown frame could be reinvented as a sort of Disneyland, with each "land" offering a different at-traction. In some downtowns, including San Diego, much of the surrounding land was successfully set aside for the creation of residential neighborhoods. In a few years, the image of living downtown changed dramatically from one dominated by skid row hotels to one characterized by skyscraping condos and trendy bistros.

The redevelopment, or perhaps more accurately reinvention, of downtown San Diego only took off in the 1980s with the open-ing of Horton Plaza Shopping Center. The colorful, postmodern million-square-foot mall not only attracted shoppers to the down-town for the first time in decades, but also bolstered the strug-gling Gaslamp Quarter Historic District on adjacent streets.[19] With a large parking garage and the relatively familiar surroundings of anchor stores, more people were willing to venture into the bars and jazz clubs that were springing up on the once grungy streets of the former skid row. Downtown was becoming a happening place by the late 1980s. Still, people were only beginning to move there during that decade.

Meanwhile, the waterfront was gradually being rediscovered and access to the amenity improved. As industrial activities and the Navy gradually decamped from the downtown waterfront, recreational and commercial uses were developed to take their place. Seaport Village, a complex of shops and restaurants using an Early California architectural theme, appeared in the late 1970s, and for the first time, there was a real, although not necessarily authentic, multipurpose attraction next to the water. A waterfront park and a marina were soon built nearby and strolling along the Bay became a major San Diego pastime. But no residences were permitted along the Bay. In 1962, all the land in downtown San Diego that fronted the Bay was put under the jurisdiction of the newly created San Diego Unified Port District. The idea was to coordinate activity all around the Bay, which was then controlled by five individual cities—San Diego, National City, Chula Vista, Imperial Beach, and Coronado. Rules were put into effect that only profitable land uses such as airports, ship terminals, hotels, and commercial projects could be built on land controlled by the Port. The fact that the waterfront was off limits for housing probably delayed the advent of downtown residential neighborhoods.

Still, things began to change during the late 1980s. With the success of the Gaslamp Quarter, Seaport Village, Horton Plaza, and other amenity destinations, the image of downtown as a boring, somewhat sleazy area was turned around. Downtown became a place for tourists and dazzling urbanites. This was especially true after the opening of the new convention center and Marriott Hotel towers along the waterfront in 1989. Even with all the new developments, however, there was still a lot of empty space in the two-square-mile central core. After an office building miniboom came to an end in the mid-1980s, it became apparent that some other land uses were needed if downtown was ever going to be developed to its full potential. The city, or more specifically the Centre City Development Corporation (CCDC), turned its attention to the creation of downtown residential neighborhoods. There were at least four reasons why this strategy seemed to be a viable option. First, downtown had become a major full-service urban center with a significant amount of office employment as well as shopping, dining, and cultural attractions. Second, downtown was seen as well located for recreation and amenities since it was squeezed between Balboa Park and the newly accessible waterfront. Third, the very high cost of housing in San Diego meant that condominiums costing $400,000 and up were not out of the question and building on valuable downtown land made economic sense. Finally, San Diego was attracting large numbers of people who had lived in big cities all their lives and were attracted to a downtown lifestyle. At least some former New Yorkers and Bostonians preferred downtown to life at the beach, even though, as one person remarked, it was really only a "toy downtown."

By 1990, downtown had a population of 15,484 and for the first time at least one downtown neighborhood had an average income equal to that of the city as a whole. Downtown living was becoming normal. About 200 single-family houses still remained, many converted to commercial uses, but there were no contiguous neighborhoods of old houses still intact. High- and medium-density condominiums and apartment buildings were becoming the norm. After a four-year hiatus caused by the severe economic downturn in California during the early 1990s, the downtown housing boom really took off.

The job of building a residential downtown was perhaps too big and too new to be handled by local builders alone. Developers from other parts of the world, especially the Bosa Corporation from Vancouver, were brought in to build towers aimed at the luxury market. In addition, a variety of colorful mid-rise complexes, converted industrial lofts, and townhouse projects were introduced, often for the first time in San Diego. New kinds of marketing strategies evolved to sell the idea of urban living, featuring images often borrowed from New York and Chicago, but neighborhood-specific themes have also played an important role in promoting the concept of an urbane lifestyle.

Inventing Downtown Theme Districts

As the downtown frame was carved up into different theme districts, five distinctive residential neighborhoods emerged, each with its own character and appeal: the Marina District, Little Italy, Cortez Hill, the Gaslamp Quarter, and East Village. The Marina District, so named because it is located in what had been a waterfront warehouse area that is now dominated by Seaport Village, Marina Park, and major convention hotels, was the first area to be selected for residential construction. With the attraction of shops and restaurants at Seaport Village and a green park lined with sailboats, it was easy to sell the area as an amenity-rich neighborhood. Two condo projects opened in 1980, both low-rise, suburban style developments with about 200 units each that were aimed at making people feel comfortable downtown. Over time, the architectural styles changed and became a bit more urban in character, although still largely low-rise, with more doors at street level and fewer parking garage entryways. Today, however, the area boasts luxury towers of more than forty stories with several more in the twenty- to thirty-story range. There are also a number of new low- and mid-rise projects with a more urban look. The district is just about finished, with nearly all the available lots covered with housing. There were six projects under construction in 2002, with between 200 and 400 units each; two of the largest

CHAPTER 3

New high-density residences in the downtown Marina District.

towers are set to open in 2005. The appeal is access to downtown shopping, waterfront parks, sailboats, Seaport Village, and the waterside promenades associated with the convention facilities and major hotels.

Several blocks to the north of the Marina District, on the northern side of the urban core, Little Italy exudes a somewhat different sense of place. Just as the name "Marina District" helped in the revitalization of that area, the term "Little Italy" has served to focus attention and investment there. This section of the downtown frame was dubbed "Harborview" for most of the last two decades, but this name failed to generate much activity, in part because many areas have harbor views. The name Little Italy, however, provided a ready-made and largely authentic theme to build on. In the 1920s, when Italian and Portuguese fishermen first moved into this waterfront neighborhood, the area was well beyond the boundaries of the CBD. Tiny one-story cottages were the norm, with Catholic churches and small stores along the major streets. The area began to decline with the construction of Interstate 5 in the late 1950s and early 1960s. Not only were many houses and businesses destroyed, but the neighborhood was cut in two as the more commercial waterfront district was separated from the nicer houses and apartments farther up the hill toward Balboa Park. Although a few remaining churches and Italian restaurants bolstered it, the area was considered to be part of the low-income, largely Latino downtown frame by the 1960s. Most of the older housing was either poorly maintained as rentals or converted to commercial uses. No new housing was built over the fifty-year period between about 1930 and 1980, and few residents claimed Italian descent.

New restaurants began to appear during the affluent 1980s, but Little Italy began to take off as a desirable residential neighborhood only in the mid-1990s. The theme was played to the hilt. A large banner across India Street in the heart of the district and decorative signs and flags on light poles vividly proclaimed the "Italianness" of the neighborhood. Pictures of famous Italian Americans such as Frank Sinatra and Rudolph Guiliani found a place on the poles for a while, replaced by seasonal Buon Natale signs at Christmas. The sidewalks were repaved with colorful stone and vest pocket parks were added. By the late 1990s, dozens of new housing projects were underway. These projects, however, differ markedly from those in the Marina District.

Little Italy is not far from the flight path into Lindbergh Field International Airport and so the kind of urbane towers found in the Marina District are out of the question except at the southern edge of the area. There it is possible to go up to just over twenty stories or about 250 feet. In addition, the colorful, street-level sense of fun that has been used to sell the image of the area does not go very well with monumental towers. Little Italy has therefore emphasized a combination of mid-rise, often mixed-use structures with Mediterranean color schemes and industrial-chic loft buildings and row houses. Both styles reference a kind of lifestyle associated with the Little Italys of larger cities such as New York

Little Italy is a reinvented residential neighborhood in downtown San Diego.

and San Francisco. This neighborhood is becoming famous for its avant-garde and otherwise unusual architecture. Cafes and shops line the streets and a burgeoning art district adds to the Bohemian ambience. Rents are not as high as in the tallest Marina District towers, but they are too high to facilitate the authentic kind of Little Italy being emulated. Still, the area has become a well-known and highly imageable place in downtown San Diego. In late 2002 there were thirteen major residential projects underway, many with Italian names such as Bella Via, La Piazza, Allegro Tower, and La Vita.

Several neighborhood names have been used for the area between Little Italy and the Marina District, most recently the Columbia District and Core-Columbia (after Columbia Street). Neither name has generated much interest since it is hard to identify with a nondescript street. It seems likely that the two more marketable neighborhoods will simply grow together into a "greater waterfront" residential district. Plans call for residential towers of up to thirty-nine stories around the increasingly busy train station and adjacent to the CBD office core.

But the waterfront is not the only game in town. Cortez Hill, named after the 1928 El Cortez Hotel that occupies its pinnacle, lies to the northeast of the central business district. This was once the "zone of assimilation" or nicer part of the downtown frame since it was uphill from the busy waterfront and largely residential. The original attraction was a location adjacent to the amenity of Balboa Park before the Interstate was pushed through in the early 1960s. The freeway cut off the hill from the park and left it in an isolated but relatively serene corner of the urban core. With the famous hotel acting as an anchor, the first tentative attempts to build new middle-income apartment complexes were made here during the early 1970s. When the El Cortez Hotel closed in the late 1970s, the entire neighborhood went into a tailspin. After various unsuccessful attempts to revive the hotel or convert it to other uses, the area was slated for massive redevelopment during the 1980s. Rumors of mysterious Japanese investors planning to build towering multi-use complexes on the hill appeared from time to time, but even those plans faded by the time of the early 1990s economic doldrums. When the economy picked up in the mid-1990s, Cortez Hill emerged as yet another downtown residential theme district. Lacking a waterfront or even a coherent ethnic history, the theme this time was the glory of the former El Cortez Hotel.

The hotel itself experienced many changes during its half-century of existence. The biggest changes occurred during the 1950s, when its architecture was changed from "interwar elegance" to "Las Vegas strip pizazz." The world's first outside glass elevator was installed in 1957, and the building was embellished with multicolored stars and a big neon sign. A large gull-winged, glass-enclosed restaurant and bar were added at the top of the fifteen-story tower and it soon became *the* place to go for a view over the city and bay. With black and red leather furniture and a "Ricky

Ricardo" nightclub ambience, the bar and restaurant added a touch of adventure to the relatively tame downtown.

The hotel spun off a number of motels nearby, since the district was well away from the commercial core and low buildings with free parking were feasible. Freeway access and close proximity to the San Diego Zoo and the other attractions of Balboa Park meant that the hotels and motels existed in a somewhat separate world from the business core. The El Cortez itself, however, remained one of the most popular venues for such big events as senior proms well into the 1970s. By the 1980s, however, the entire area seemed run down and sadly out of date, as big new hotels opened along the waterfront.

This area's future arrived during the mid-1990s, when developers proposed to rehabilitate the El Cortez and convert it to prewar style luxury rental apartments. The lobby and ground level shops would be returned to the elegance of former days and all the 1950s additions would be removed except for the large red El Cortez sign at the top. The plan worked. The El Cortez became a prestigious theme building for the new residential district. By the year 2000, several other projects were underway with the largest being the twenty-four-story, 199-unit Discovery at Cortez Hill condominium tower. The developer, Bosa Corporation, built the tower in the glassy Vancouver style associated with the many new residential towers in that city. It may turn out that there is too much sun in San Diego for such an open style, but the views are great if you can stand the glare. At present, there are ten residential projects in Cortez Hill including everything from row houses to towers.

San Diego's former skid row became the Gaslamp Quarter during the 1980s, and today it has scores of restaurants and shops that appeal to locals and tourists alike. The Marina District abuts the Gaslamp and the line between the two is fuzzy but, in general, towers are discouraged within the official historic district. Therefore, a variety of smaller residential projects are currently being inserted into this lively area. Most of these are either lofts in renovated buildings or mid-rise structures designed to blend into the overall ambience of the place. The serenity of Cortez Hill is completely absent in the Gaslamp Quarter. Indeed, one of the main issues facing residents is dealing with the loud music and boisterous behavior emanating from the many clubs and nightspots in San Diego's premier entertainment strip. Before the Gaslamp became popular, several retirement complexes were either built or renovated in the area, but it is not an area known for quiet reflection. Today it may be one of the best examples of a lifestyle zone in the city. Street level retail and entertainment are ubiquitous, and so getting away from it all is not easy. The six residential projects currently underway in the Gaslamp area all feature units that are close to the action, sometimes just above the bars and cafes.

The downtown core or central business district and all four of the largely residential subdistricts discussed so far make up only about half of what is now considered downtown San Diego. Downtown has twenty-six north-south streets with half west and half east of the Gaslamp Quarter's main drag, Fifth Avenue. So far, most of the action has been west of Fifth, or at least west of Eighth. Nearly a square mile of the downtown remains very lightly developed.

For most of its history, the eastern edge of downtown as a whole had no name, although several attempts have been made to give identity to parts of it. Today, however, the entire area is known as East Village in an attempt to reference urban districts elsewhere, particularly New York. South of San Diego City (community) College, most of the district consists of small houses, one-story warehouses, parking lots, and a few small commercial strips. During the 1980s, art galleries, coffee houses, and loft residences began to appear in what was then being termed an art district, but the efforts were only partly successful and many closed or operated only on a part-time basis.

Part of the problem is the existence of large numbers of poverty-related services in the area. With the renovation of the old skid row into the Gaslamp Quarter, all the homeless shelters, soup kitchens, and other poverty-linked operations were pushed eastward. There are often long lines for food and shelter in front of the rescue missions, and this adds to the negative image of the area. Accurate estimates are difficult to come by, but it is generally agreed that at least 5,500 homeless people roam the streets of San Diego, and a high percentage of them spend at least some time in East Village. About 1,500 people, for example, are normally housed in shelters such as the three-building St. Vincent de Paul Center at Fifteenth and Imperial Avenue and the nearby San Diego Rescue Mission. In addition, temporary tent shelters are usually put up during the winter months. Owners of galleries that closed often suggested that people sleeping in doorways were a significant factor in their decisions.

The major geographic problem in the East Village is simply that the district is too big and lacks any significant node or sense of center, other than the college on the northern edge. Two big projects are in the works to change this situation. The first, open as of April 2004, is the San Diego Padres baseball stadium. Again following the lead of well-known projects in other cities, San Diego (after many heated discussions, law suits, and scandals) has created an old-fashioned "Camden Yards" style ballpark in the southwestern corner of East Village in close proximity to the Gaslamp Quarter and convention center. The ballpark is intended to be not only a major downtown attraction, but a "big footprint" structure that absorbs excess space and gives a focus and scarcity value to nearby East Village blocks. The park itself takes up over ten blocks and adjacent redevelopment projects add about ten more. Thus, in one fell swoop, nearly one-third of the "empty"

East Village space has been utilized. A new residential district is going up in the "Ballpark District." A dozen residential projects, including renovated lofts and new condominium towers are under construction in the immediate vicinity of the ballpark. This is another lifestyle zone in the making, since traffic, noise, and a certain amount of chaos are sure to be evident on game days. Controversies over lifestyle have already arisen: new plans to build taller buildings around the ballpark have angered many of the pioneer residents who sought a funky loft and baseball neighborhood with a less corporate look.

The second major project that will affect the East Village is the "Park to Bay" grand boulevard planned, at long last, to link Balboa Park to San Diego Bay, or at least the ballpark. The boulevard will follow the Park Boulevard-Twelfth Avenue path and provide a monumental "main street" for East Village that if successful will be an attraction for even more residential development.

San Diego has now emerged as one of the top ten cities in America for both the size and status of its downtown residential population. After the handful of "major players" such as New York, Chicago, Boston, San Francisco, and Philadelphia, San Diego is vying with Seattle to be the leader of the second tier cities in the realm of downtown living.[20] The problem is that almost all the new housing has been upscale. In its quest to emulate "big league" cities in the provision of penthouse suites (ads for the new places sometimes feature champagne-sipping couples in formal attire), the issue of affordable housing has been placed on the back burner. While some low-end housing has appeared as the result of new regulations requiring such units in return for permission to build large projects, the numbers are minimal. Housing advocates hope that more modest projects will some day be constructed in what remains of East Village, but even this idea is fading in light of the wildly inflated San Diego housing market. By the year 2020, when downtown achieves its goal of 50,000 residents, chances are it will be a place for dazzling urbanites and the soup kitchens will be long gone.

MISSION VALLEY: MIDTOWN, EDGE CITY, OR BOTH?

One of the best examples of a physically defined community in San Diego lies less than three miles north of downtown. Despite its proximity to the central city, Mission Valley was nearly devoid of urban development until the 1960s. It consists of a nearly flat flood plain about six miles long and less than half a mile wide. Its steep sides and flat bottom were formed over the millennia by the San Diego River as it meandered from the mountains to the Bay, and later because of channeling, to the ocean. For nearly a century, Mission Valley was the home of farms, dairies, and sand and gravel mining. It was a rural landscape just below the streetcar suburbs on the cliffs above.

The Valley's tardy development was due primarily to two things; the difficulty of getting to it by public transportation and the danger of periodic flooding. The first problem was largely overcome by the mid-1960s with the construction of Interstate 8 through the valley coupled with widespread automobile ownership. The access roads in and out of the Valley had always been far too steep for streetcars and even early buses, but automobiles could handle the grade, although some, such as my old Volkswagen van, had some difficulty. By the early 1960s, freeway frontage roads provided ideal locations for space-extensive shopping malls, motels, convention facilities, and sports complexes since there was plenty of empty and affordable land in the Valley surrounded by residential mesas filled with eager consumers. By 1970, Mission Valley had two of the largest shopping malls in the county as well as the largest convention center and the major all-purpose stadium. It also contained a variety of car dealerships, drive-through restaurants, movie theaters, office parks, and nightclubs. As a result, Mission Valley became a major but somewhat confusing destination. With only two east-west highways, I-8 and Friars Road, rush hour congestion gradually became a problem as the Valley filled in. Also, big footprint developments such as shopping centers meant that there was a sparse network of secondary streets. Getting from one side of the freeway to the other was especially problematic.

Even with the new highways, development in Mission Valley was premature. Huge floods had occurred in 1916 and 1927 with water covering the entire valley floor, so for a long time most developers avoided the Valley. The construction of upriver dams ameliorated the problem to a limited extent, but floods continued to inundate the area periodically and the damage increased along with urban development. The last major deluge came in 1980, when several roads and even the first dozen rows in a major theater were underwater. Most but not all construction was carried out with an awareness of the danger. Many buildings were built as far back from the river as possible, but a surprising number of the largest structures were built very close. Some of these, such as Mission Valley Shopping Center, had open underground parking garages that theoretically would experience minimal damage in the event of a flood. Other structures were built on artificial berms, a good solution for small floods but not big ones.[21]

Much of the land that was most flood-prone was zoned for recreation, mainly golf courses—a use that complemented nearby hotels. In general, developers simply decided that the location was so good in terms of accessibility that they would take the risk. Even the *Union-Tribune*, the city's major newspaper, left downtown for a more centrally located site in Mission Valley. If a business that specialized in information moved to the Valley, how dangerous could it be? On the other hand, many felt that once enough investment had been committed to Mission Valley, a strong argument could be made for major expenditures for flood protection. Chief among these was a concrete flood channel similar to those in Los Angeles.

Needless to say, the prospect of a massive concrete channel was controversial. Such a channel would almost guarantee that most flooding could be controlled, but the cost was immense and floods the size of the one that occurred in 1916 might still inundate the Valley. In addition, concrete channels are usually horrendously ugly, especially since they are dry most of the time. The Los Angeles channels, for example, are aesthetic disamenities that do little to enhance nearby property values. In addition, conservationists argued against the total elimination of any semblance of a riparian landscape along the historic San Diego River. In 1976, the Army Corps of Engineers ruled that a concrete flood channel was not a viable option for Mission Valley since federal funding for such a project could not be economically justified. The cost-effectiveness of other more "natural" options was explored.

The floods of 1978 and 1980 caused millions of dollars of damage in Mission Valley, and it was clear that something had to be done. By the late 1980s, a natural appearing, "soft bottom" channel was created and paid for by property owners. The disadvantage of this solution is that the channel cannot handle the largest possible floods. The advantage is that it provides a much-needed natural amenity in the increasingly traffic-clogged Valley. The river is now lined with pathways and vegetation and is heavily used by joggers and strollers. In many places it provides the only pedestrian friendly walkway for miles around. It has become a magnet for new development.

Mission Valley experienced a boom during the 1990s. In addition to the usual commercial land uses such as shopping centers, big box retailing, and office towers, there was now housing. Most of the area was zoned for mixed use, meaning that housing, theaters, shopping, offices, and medical complexes could be put to-

Highways, shopping malls, and thousands of new housing units in Mission Valley.

gether in ways that had not been seen for many decades. Massive apartment and condominium complexes appeared between the malls, hotels, and golf courses. The sprawling suburban landscape started to fill in as some of the disparate parts were knitted together.[22]

Things have also begun to change on the transportation front. A light rail system is currently (2004) being built through the eastern extension of the Valley. During the late 1990s the line was extended from downtown and Old Town to Qualcomm Stadium through the heart of the Mission Valley commercial district. People going from nearby hotels to shopping centers or a football game could avoid the awkward road network by taking the train. The rail line also connects to Tijuana and the South Bay through downtown San Diego, although it is a long trip. When the line is completed to San Diego State University and on to the suburb of La Mesa where it will connect to existing lines to both eastern suburbs and downtown, Mission Valley will become one of the most centrally located nodes in the region. Commuters will travel from the eastern suburbs and tourists will come from downtown hotels by rail as well as by car.

Mission Valley is now what Joel Garreau has called an Edge City, a suburban district with a full range of shopping, office, entertainment, and recreational activities reasonably well linked together in one place.[23] Mission Valley vies with downtown and the La Jolla-Sorrento Valley area for being the largest single employment center in the county. It dominates the retail landscape with two giant malls and several smaller ones that with about four million square feet of space make it the metropolitan area's largest shopping destination. The term Edge City does not adequately describe Mission Valley geographically, however, because it is very close to the population center of the county. It is not on the edge of anything. It is probably best described as a kind of "Midtown" in common with, say, the Wilshire corridor in Los Angeles or the Peachtree spine in Atlanta. It is very close to the old downtown but has a completely separate identity. It is quintessentially both urban and suburban depending on where you stand.

Mission Valley has also become a very important and distinctive residential community in San Diego. The theme increasingly is a combination of transit-oriented development and mixed-use urban living. Unlike downtown, however, the housing in Mission Valley is all new, or at least recent, and there are no scruffy older districts awaiting redevelopment or preservation. Everything, and to some degree everyone, is very much the same. For our purposes, it qualifies as a lifestyle zone. Approximately 10,000 people live in Mission Valley, virtually all of them in large, low-rise condominium and apartment complexes. Unlike downtown, Mission Valley is not a center for architectural innovation or high-rise luxury living. Most units are in sprawling beige, red-tiled complexes with several hundred apartments. The costs for both buying and renting a unit are pretty close to the county mean since there are no older marginal areas or new luxury towers. The goal is to have about 25,000 residents in the area by the time the Valley is totally built out.

The census tracts do not match up well with the Valley since most extend into northern neighborhoods. Still, it is clear that most (about 80 percent) residents are non-Hispanic whites who are either young or empty nesters. Mission Valley is an adult community that sells access to malls, restaurants, fitness clubs, golf courses, movie theaters, jogging trails, and entertainment hot spots. There are no schools in Mission Valley and recent plans to increase the density of the area, as part of a "city of villages" scheme, did not call for any. There are also very few parks or playgrounds in the traditional sense.

While residential development has tended to hug the river in recent years, most of the complexes are scattered over a wide area and intermixed with commercial projects, so there is little sense of neighborhood. It is a very convenient place to live and one that emphasizes a sort of social neutrality. There is relatively little pressure to fit in, despite the architectural and demographic homogeneity. Turnover is relatively high and many condominium units are rentals. Single person households are also quite common. As downtown becomes more specialized, Mission Valley is a place for new residents to land and "learn the ropes" in San Diego.

A place like Mission Valley is much needed in the San Diego Metropolitan Area. Despite the fact that nearly half the residents in San Diego County are renters, only about 8 percent of the developable land currently zoned for residential uses is slated for multi-unit projects. Neighborhoods throughout the region have organized to stop the construction of apartments and condominiums in single-family communities. Because Mission Valley is zoned for mixed use with residential uses plunked down between malls and office parks, opposition to new projects is minimal. On the other hand, unlike the case in Ocean Beach, no one has "I Love MV" stickers on their cars either.

LIFE IN CENTRAL SAN DIEGO

It is common in the United States to think of urban areas divided between central or even "inner" cities and suburbs. Within the central city, the story goes, diversity is usually a function of ethnicity or social class. Anyone who has watched the New York Marathon on television knows of the tremendous ethnic collage that makes up the various neighborhoods and boroughs of the city. Similarly, we have long been told of the "Gold Coast and Slum" economic divides in central cities. In this chapter, however, I have examined several centrally located neighborhoods with the aim of looking at them as a series of very different kinds of places or lifestyle zones even when ethnicity and economic status are held constant. In North American cities, and especially in San Diego, people are increasingly seeking individual identity through place identity. Theme villages complete with icons and symbols allow people to choose a way of life that goes beyond activities associated with income and education.

If anything, I have greatly understated the situation in central San Diego. In addition to Ocean Beach, Sherman Heights, Kensington, Downtown, and Mission Valley, there are at least a dozen other highly individualistic communities in the central city. Among them are Mission Beach, Pacific Beach, Hillcrest, North Park, Skyline, College, Point Loma, and Mission Hills. The combination of topographical separation, variations in architecture and vegetation, and real estate and local business promotions has made identification with a distinctive place an important dimension of choosing a place to live in central San Diego.

CHAPTER FOUR

Lifestyle Zones on the Edge of Town

The neighborhoods of central San Diego are extremely diverse
but those in the suburban ring fifteen to twenty miles out are
even more varied. The range of lifestyles associated with this
ring boggles the mind. Fifteen miles south of downtown San
Diego, for example, is the city of Tijuana, Mexico with its roughly
1.5 million people. Although not technically part of the metropolitan area, it is connected to San Diego in so many ways—as we
have seen—that it is absurd to ignore it in any discussion of the
greater San Diego region. Fifteen miles north of downtown is La
Jolla, one of the richest neighborhoods in the county, with the
average house priced at well over a million dollars. Actually a
part of the city of San Diego, La Jolla is known throughout the
nation as a unique and charming place. It is hard to imagine a
social or cultural gradient steeper than the one between La Jolla
and Tijuana.

Beginning about twenty miles east of downtown, there is a
string of eighteen Native American reservations, now thriving with
casinos, outlet malls, and other attractions. A number of more
traditionally suburban locales are interspersed among these out-
liers, ranging from small towns like La Mesa to giant planned unit
developments like Eastlake. This chapter explores five very different kinds of residential areas in this suburban ring.

LA JOLLA: IDYLLIC ENCLAVE AND BUSTLING EDGE CITY

At first glance, the "urban problems" associated with the village of La Jolla do not seem to be earth shattering by North American standards. One of the big issues, for example, is whether or not California sea lions should have the right to permanently occupy what since 1931 has been a breakwater-enclosed children's swimming area at La Jolla Cove. So far, the sea lions have won the day. Another controversial issue is whether or not déclassé restaurants like McDonald's should be allowed in the village where "people can occupy valuable space for the price of a Big Mac." Another burning issue is whether to allow a forty-three-foot concrete cross, ostensibly a war memorial, to dominate the top of Mount Soledad. The solution, so far, has been to sell the site of the cross to private owners so that it is no longer on public land, even though it still sits in the middle of a park.

At Black's Beach, just north of Old La Jolla, residents have wrestled with the issue of whether the cliff-faced, hard-to-get to sandy strip should be a legally designated a "free" or nude beach. So far, the designation has been on-again, off-again just like the bathing suits. These issues and others such as sign control and architectural guidelines occupy a considerable amount of civic energy. Even though La Jolla has always been, since the initial establishment of city boundaries in 1870, a neighborhood within the city of San Diego, movements aimed at succession have arisen on several occasions. Some La Jollans feel that the place would be better off with local, more exclusive government, so that even arcane issues could be dealt with seriously. Bitter battles have been fought (successfully) over La Jolla's right to have its own post office and postmark so that letters can be addressed to La Jolla rather than San Diego. Like residents of Ocean Beach, La Jollans feel strongly about defining and defending a local identity, but in most ways the two communities could not be more different. La Jollans see their community as a luxurious setting with an urbane, international flavor. Such things as beachfront amusement parks and roller coasters were never part of the local sense of place.

On the other hand, there are some real problems in La Jolla. Chief among them is traffic congestion. With very few ways to get in and out of the village, cars line up for a mile at rush hour. The widespread desire to be as close as possible to the prestigious and famous neighborhood and bask in its fame and glory creates an attractive nuisance. Office parks, shopping centers, medical and research complexes, and high-density condominium communities now occupy every inch of available land all around the original village of La Jolla. Indeed, the number of La Jolla signs may be greater outside the village than in it as everyone tries to establish a link to the famous name. Consequently, it is increasingly difficult to determine exactly what and where La Jolla is. There are no consensus official boundaries, so a wide range of disparate communities such as Mount Soledad, Sorrento Valley, and University Town Center all identify with being part of a rather nebulous "greater La Jolla." Many argue that too much success will kill La Jolla's identity and charm as it moves away from being a village and becomes the center of a giant, sprawling edge city.

Part of La Jolla's independent spirit derives from the fact that it is nearly as well known around the country, and maybe the world, as San Diego itself. It is now, and has always been, a tourist destination in its own right. La Jolla, along with the nearby Del Mar race track, has been a popular destination for people from Los Angeles for over a century. With the advent of automobiles and paved roads, Hollywood celebrities came south in droves for the racing season during the 1920s and 1930s and stayed at posh hotels such as the Valencia in La Jolla. Most never ventured further south into the heart of San Diego. Today, tourists come from all over the world; it is sometimes difficult to find anyone speaking English while strolling along Prospect Street on a summer evening.

Although many people know the name La Jolla, not everyone knows what it means or even how to pronounce it. The most popular explanation of the name is that it is derived from "La Joya," meaning jewel in Spanish. This definition conforms closest to the image locals would like to sell, but it does not explain the unusual spelling. Others claim that the name comes from La Hoya (more correctly El Hoyo), meaning hollow or cave, a common feature at La Jolla Cove, where, in spite of serious erosion in recent decades, cliffs, arches, and caves abound. Still others argue that words from Native American languages inspired the name. Local Indians called the place Woholle, which may have entered Spanish as Jolla. Still others say that the name is derived from "olla," water jug, and that early seamen gave the name to the whirlpools at La Jolla Cove. All that is really important today is that the word is pronounced as though the J were an H and the two Ls a Y.

La Jolla: The Physical Setting

The main attraction in La Jolla is now and always has been its unique physical setting. There is no other place on the southern California coast like it. A promontory jutting into the Pacific basically defines the original locale known as La Jolla. The northern shore of the promontory contains the caves, arches, monumental rocks, exposed (at low tide) rocks, and steep cliffs that made La Jolla Cove a place worth visiting as early as the 1870s. Just to the north of the Cove, the sandy beaches of La Jolla Shores provide a more traditional seashore ambience. In addition, the 350-foot cliffs at Black's Beach and the 800-foot "mountain" known as Mount Soledad provide a sense of enclosure that historically gave the area well-defined boundaries and a strong sense of identity.

At low tide, it is possible to explore the tide pools and rocky crevices and stretch out on the unusual rock slabs. At high tide, monumental waves can come crashing over the rocks and seawall contributing to a wild, dangerous, and awesome coastal scene. For a long time, it was not easy to get to La Jolla. Although it was widely known as a beautiful spot as early as the 1870s, there were few ways to get there from San Diego. One visitor described the journey as a "long and dusty fourteen mile ride behind a pair of the scraggiest mules under the hottest midday sun."[1] La Jolla was little more than a scenic place for noontime picnics, since it took at least four hours to get there. There were a few attempts at development, such as a subdivision known as La Jolla Park, but they came to very little until the boom of the late 1880s. Even then, little happened. There was a brisk sale of lots in 1887, but the crash of 1888 brought everything to a halt and by 1890 most of the investors had lost money and interest. As late as 1896, residential lots were valued at about ten dollars and only a few "hotel-cottages" had been built. The Green Dragon Colony, twelve cottages built as an artist retreat from 1894 to 1902 (since destroyed) became one of the community's first architectural landmarks. In 1900 the population was put, perhaps optimistically, at 350.

Since La Jolla was part of the City of San Diego and technically dependent upon it for services such as water, roads, and sewers, investment in infrastructure was more complicated than it might have been if the village could have incorporated as a separate town. It would be years before any services would arrive. The first water pipe was constructed by the city in the 1890s, but it only provided water at night. Wells were used to supply the rest. The problem was solved only in 1919 with a contract between San Diego and the San Dieguito Mutual Water Company.

Access to the area improved in 1894 when the San Diego and Pacific Beach Railroad extended a line into La Jolla. The steam

La Jolla Cove.

train service lasted until 1919. By the mid-1920s, paved roads made travel by automobile and motorbus possible, but of course cars also brought traffic. In 1925, the *La Jolla Journal* reported that cars were passing through the village on the old coast road at a rate of 1,160 per hour. Much of this early through traffic was eliminated when U.S. Highway 101 was built on the east side of Mount Soledad in 1930, bypassing La Jolla. Interstate 5 took the same route in 1966. There was an alternative during the 1920s, since for a while a "modern" express electric streetcar line also connected La Jolla to the outside world. By then, the remote picnic spot and tent city resort had evolved into a viable community with a golf course, elite girls' school, luxurious hotels, hospital, and "unique and distinctive architecture." A tourist brochure pointed out that "fully fifty persons [of a total population of 4,000–5,000] of national or sectional prominence make their homes in La Jolla." La Jolla already had the distinctive identity and character that would help it gradually evolve into an early version of an American Edge City, complete with a full range of economic and cultural attractions.

The La Jolla Incubator

It is tough for La Jolla to have it both ways. On the one hand, it has struggled to retain its image as a quaint village that never changes; and on the other, it has struggled to develop an image of high fashion, culture, and scientific innovation. It is a complex centrifugal machine—a tiny village continuously spinning off big, space extensive activities. These issues began to take shape during the 1920s, when La Jolla overflowed to the north (La Jolla Shores), south (Birdrock), and east (up the slopes of Mount Soledad). How big could La Jolla be without losing its identity and charm?

The village of La Jolla also experienced significant rebuilding during the 1920s as small resort cottages were replaced by larger commercial buildings, apartment blocks, and hotels. Some people called for zoning laws and architectural guidelines while others argued against any kind of limit on free enterprise, especially if it came from "outsiders" such as the San Diego City Council. Things slowed down during the Depression and World War II, but by the 1940s there were major issues that had to be addressed. La Jolla was becoming too popular. In order to keep the village from turning into a Coney Island or Atlantic City, the Architectural Control League of La Jolla was formed in 1947. Its purpose was to (strongly) suggest appropriate architectural styles to interested developers.

By the 1950s and 1960s, La Jolla was facing development issues that were far more pronounced, if not completely different, from those in most other elite suburban enclaves. The problem, in a nutshell, was that La Jolla was too successful at creating world famous independent institutions that constantly needed room for expansion. These institutions were usually founded in the village, but there was little room there for expansion, and so a continuous round of "move or rebuild" battles developed. An early example of this is provided by Scripps Hospital. Ellen Browning Scripps moved to La Jolla with her ailing brother E. W. in 1897 and purchased land in what was to become the heart of the village. Through generous contributions of land and money over the decades, the Scripps family name has become a part of many local institutions such as the Scripps Institute of Oceanography, Scripps Memorial Hospital, Scripps Park, and Scripps Institution for Biological Research. Perhaps the story begins in 1922 when Ellen Scripps broke her hip and found the hospital facilities in La Jolla inadequate. By 1924 there was a new and larger hospital in the middle of town—Scripps Memorial. As the hospital grew and expanded, it was clear that it would have to be relocated. The latest incarnation is a massive complex built in the mid-1970s four miles north of the village on Torrey Pines Boulevard. This and several similar stories go a long way toward explaining La Jolla's development. Rich and powerful people found that the community was too attractive to leave but too isolated from San Diego for access to needed facilities, and so they created independent institutions that attracted more rich and powerful people to the village. The list is a long one. The Scripps Institute of Oceanography moved to La Jolla Shores, where new facilities have been expanded over the years. The La Jolla Playhouse, started by local resident Gregory Peck and others in 1947, is now located on the campus of UC San Diego north of the village. The same story holds for a variety of luxurious hotels, shopping venues, and research laboratories such as the (Jonas) Salk Institute. Only a few successful ventures, such as the La Jolla Museum of Contemporary Art, have managed to stay in the village, and then only with the help of a special Cultural Overlay Zone.

The new role that La Jolla plays in San Diego became evident in 1960 with the establishment of the University of California, San Diego (originally to be called UC La Jolla) campus on the site of the former Camp Callan military base four miles north of the village. The campus soon became known for medical, biological, and oceanographic research (in association with the preexisting Scripps facilities) and now serves as the focus for what seems to be an unending number of high-tech office parks and labs. Very little of this activity takes place in what has been traditionally known as La Jolla, but at the same time it is very closely associated with the paradisiacal and glamorous image of the place. Medical doctors, scientists, artists, and computer wizards have come in droves to be part of the La Jolla lifestyle, even though they may rarely have time to get to the original village. Torrey Pines Mesa, University City, Sorrento Valley, and the eastern slope of Mount Soledad are all thought to be part of greater La

Luxury housing on the slopes of Mount Soledad.

Jolla even though they are very different kinds of places. Indeed, there is even a community called La Jolla Village a few miles away from what is still known as the village of La Jolla. The name is important. It attracts Nobel Prize winners and medical expertise. Meanwhile, the original La Jolla is doing its best to remain charming even in the face of rampant change. High rise buildings made their first appearance in the early 1960s, but they are no longer allowed. Big footprint buildings that need lots of more than about 10,000 square feet are also nearly impossible to build. The combination of restrictive zoning and architectural controls has kept at least some of the charm intact, even though a number of historical landmarks have been replaced by bigger business buildings over the years. The fact that about half the original buildings in the village of La Jolla had been replaced by 1980 led to the La Jolla Planned District Ordinance in 1984, which has all but banned large, boxy buildings. Still, space is valuable and rents are high, and most of the shops are art galleries, fine restaurants, jewelry stores, real estate offices, banks, or high-end clothing shops. Tourists and day-tripping visitors account for much of the sales volume as "everyday need" stores" have gradually decamped. The main regional shopping venue is now the University Town Center Mall (1974), located well to the east in what is known as the Golden Triangle but on a street named La Jolla Village Drive.

What and Where Is La Jolla

According to the City of San Diego, the official boundaries of La Jolla, at least for planning purposes, currently enclose about 30,000 people and occupy about six square miles. There are 10,000 more people in the adjacent and closely linked communities of Torrey Pines and La Jolla Village. Over 40,000 more live in University City, an overflow shopping, medical, office, and research center that, together with Sorrento Valley, is now one of the three major employment centers in the San Diego region. Whatever it is called, the "Greater La Jolla spin-off region" is an edge city par excellence that has surpassed downtown San Diego in office employment. UC San Diego adds 20,000 students to the mix, as well as a bit of diversity to what otherwise would be a very racially homogeneous community.

Only about 7,000 people live in and around the original La Jolla settlement with its quaint village atmosphere. Most of the others live in sprawling, hilltop homes or vast apartment and condominium complexes adjacent to I-5 or the university. Over half the people in the village are renters and, while the rents are very high, many are older and seasonal. There is still a resort and retirement dimension to Old La Jolla. On Mount Soledad, however, renters make up only about 10 percent of the households (compared to a citywide average of about 50 percent) and the houses sell for well over a million dollars, with an occasional outlier going for as much as $25 million.

Most of La Jolla is very white. About 1 percent of old La Jolla is

University Town Center, an "edge city" spin-off near La Jolla.

African American, with about 5 percent Latino. Between 1960 and 1980, there was a 60 percent drop in the African American population as affordable beach cottages from the early days were redeveloped for higher and better uses, and nearly all lower income people were displaced. On the slopes of Mount Soledad, the minority percentages are similar, with about 90 percent of the people classified as non-Hispanic white. On the other hand, the neighborhood with student housing immediately adjacent to UCSD is about 75 percent minority, with two-thirds of the residents classified as Asian. And so there are different kinds of La Jolla neighborhoods, even though they all identify with the uneasy mixture of new (high-tech, biomedical, Nobel Prize winning, innovative, foreign—or at least out-of-state) and old (quaint, small, resort, easy-going, surfing, local, white) La Jolla.

The struggle to preserve, create, reinvent, and otherwise maintain an idyllic lifestyle in a unique physical setting goes on, even in the face of hyperdevelopment, skyrocketing housing costs, and terrible traffic. When people speak of highly skilled in-migrants seeking a lotus land in the golden state of California, La Jolla usually appears near the top of the list. Everything is changing even as nothing is changing. La Jolla is a state of mind that is both stable and continuously morphing. As long as people are willing to spend huge amounts of money to buy into and actively perpetuate what they believe to be the La Jolla lifestyle, the community will be able to extend its unofficial boundaries.

TIJUANA: MEXICAN METROPOLIS OR HYBRID BORDER TOWN

Downtown San Diego lies almost exactly halfway between La Jolla and Tijuana, two equally famous but very different places. Indeed, in popular imagery, Tijuana comes close to being the polar opposite of La Jolla: chaotic, tacky, poor, and tolerant of a wide variety of landscapes and behaviors. Tijuana is all these things and much more. It is a very important part of the unofficial San Diego Metropolitan Area. San Diego-Tijuana is the busiest international border crossing in the world, even if only legal crossings are counted. Even though Tijuana is not included in the official MSA figures for San Diego, it seems silly to pretend that approximately 1.5 million people do not live next door and that thousands of people do not cross the border for a variety of purposes every day.[2]

While the border represents a major problem for intra-metropolitan interaction, neither San Diego or Tijuana would likely be as big and important as they are today without it. The tourist industries, labor markets, and industrial specializations of the two sides of the border are complementary. Over the past century, one side of the line has always supplied something the other side needs.

From the air, it appears that San Diego and Tijuana are in two entirely different climatic regions. San Diego appears relatively lush and green compared to the brown and dusty landscape of

Peripheral neighborhoods in Tijuana.

Tijuana. The contrast, of course, is due to the differing availability of water and its distribution infrastructure. While nearly every resident in San Diego has access to a faucet and hose, many neighborhoods in Tijuana must rely on water trucks and so conservation is a necessity, not an option. The two landscapes differ in many other ways as well, with much of the housing in Tijuana being self-built "squatter housing" hugging the sides of steep hills on unpaved streets. In spite of these immense differences, the two sides of the border have an increasingly complex and interwoven set of economic and social relationships.

The border was established with the Treaty of Guadalupe Hidalgo in 1848 after the Mexican-American War resulted in the U.S. takeover of California. Since almost no one lived in the border region, a straight and rather arbitrary line was drawn that ignored the local landscape. The line bisected the Tijuana River Valley, so that the city of Tijuana occupies a relatively steep-sided valley that empties onto a flat plain in the United States. The result has been a long series of problems having to do with water management and flood control. During the 1970s, for example, Mexico constructed a concrete flood channel through the city of Tijuana to allow development in the flood-prone center of town. During wet years, the channelized water flowed directly onto farms in the U.S. Eventually a "natural" flood channel was created on the northern side of the border, but issues of water quality and pollution remain.

The only requirements for the creation of the border were that it be far enough north to allow Mexican access to the Pacific via Baja California, and far enough south that all of San Diego Bay would be under U.S. control. For nearly forty years the border was without significance. Cattle ranching and Spanish language and traditions dominated both sides of the line, so it was largely invisible. Things began to change only with the arrival of the railroad in San Diego and the brief economic boom in the late 1880s, when U.S. speculators created Tijuana, then known as Zaragoza.

The village that was to become Tijuana was far more connected to the emerging North American urban system than to Central Mexico. Land transportation to Mexico City ranged from primitive to nonexistent and northern Mexico was very lightly inhabited. The Mexican government under Porfirio Diaz encouraged an open door policy for American investment and development in the north, and there has been some variation on the "free trade zone" concept in place along the border since 1885. In 1889, a North American-style plan was drawn up for a new city that contained no recognition of Mexican urban traditions. Little happened after the collapse of the boom, however, and the border town had only about 1,000 people as late as 1920. Part of the problem was that the border itself became more important as the twentieth century began. The combination of the perceived threat of Pancho Villa and other Mexican revolutionaries and the selection of San Diego as a major naval port during the Spanish-American War meant that the border had to be taken more seriously. With the advent of Prohibition in 1918, the border assumed even more importance and visibility. The U.S. border patrol only began in the 1920s, and was associated as much with Prohibition as with any real need to defend an international border.

Tijuana's image as a lively border town evolved during the roaring twenties as people from the U.S. headed south in their newly acquired automobiles for booze, casino gambling, horse racing, bull fights, shopping, and late night carousing. By 1930 Tijuana had a population of 11,000 but it was still little more than a North American tourist destination. Cantinas lined the main drag, Avenida Revolución, and there was no plaza mayor, cathedral, or other feature common in Latin American cities. Gradually the city became more traditionally Mexican as roads were built from the south and internal migration increased. The government became more concerned with the city's image and outlawed casino gambling in 1935. In the 1930s, Libertad, the first major colonia or residential neighborhood, was built outside the traditional commercial strip. The city was transformed during the 1940s and 1950s as a result of war-related labor shortages in the United States. After the Depression years of the 1930s, the U.S. found itself in need of labor for the war effort. A binational treaty was signed in 1942 that created the Bracero Program, which allowed Mexicans to work legally in the U.S. The main focus was on agricultural labor, but border cities like Tijuana increasingly became labor pools for all kinds of low-end jobs from picking crops to upholstering. The population of Tijuana soared from 22,000 in 1940 to 166,000 in 1960.

By the 1960s, the Mexican government recognized that border cities were becoming large and chaotic embarrassments. In 1959, "just send my mail to the Tijuana jail" was a popular song refrain in the U.S., and a popular image of Tijuana was a sombrero-topped tourist posing on a donkey painted to look like a zebra. The government's response during the mid-1960s was to initiate the Programa Nacional Fronterizo (PRONAF). The idea was to improve the infrastructure of border cities in order to make them attractive places for industrial investment. There were also many symbolic projects such as new boulevards and monumental border entryways. Cities like Tijuana were "spruced up" as urban planning and design gained a higher priority. In 1965, the Joint U.S.-Mexico Border Industrialization Program (BIP) added more inducements to foreign firms. As the need for Mexican labor diminished on the northern side of the border, plans were made to absorb as much as possible in the newly established industrial zones. All this was happening as North American firms began to seek a "cheap labor strategy" as a way of remaining competitive and legislation, such as the Tariff Clarification Act of 1962, allowed products assembled outside the U.S. to be imported duty free. The stage was set for the maquiladoras, labor-intensive assembly plants, that have boomed in Tijuana and other border cities over the past three decades. By the early 1980s, maquiladoras were earning over half a billion dollars a year in foreign exchange.

There is concern that Tijuana may have put too many of its eggs in one basket. The maquiladora industry has declined since 2001. Some of the decline may be due to the events of 9/11 that have made it much more difficult to cross the border, but there are deeper issues. For one thing, the phasing in of the North American Free Trade Agreement (NAFTA) has led to more tariff-free trade between the U.S. and Mexico, making border zone maquiladoras less important. Also, Japanese investments in Tijuana have declined as that country's economy has staggered. This is especially true since Japan is not part of NAFTA. In addition, some argue that Mexico has not done enough to modernize the infrastructure and skill level in border cities and that new options, such as China and India, are sometimes more competitive even if they are farther away. Still, Tijuana has become an integral part of the region's economy, and that will not change even as particular activities rise and fall. New economic relationships are continuously being explored. Tijuana may be well positioned, for example, to build a cargo airfield for the region, since sites for new airports in San Diego County are nearly impossible to find. Interstate 5 was pushed south to the main border crossing at San Ysidro during the 1960s and in the 1970s, a second border gate was created at Otay Mesa to serve the growing industrial capacity there. The daily flow of cars and trucks mushroomed. It is common to have more than a dozen lanes waiting to cross. By the mid-1970s, over 100,000 people were crossing the border each day, making it the busiest border crossing in the world. Approximately 75 million people now cross the border at Tijuana each year, most of them residents of Tijuana or San Diego.[3]

Life in Greater San Diego: Examples from Two Tijuana Neighborhoods

People cross the border for all kinds of reasons, but in order to show how residents of Tijuana participate in the greater San Diego region, I will focus on two older neighborhoods or lifestyle zones in the Mexican metropolis: Chapultepec and Libertad. Many residents in both communities cross the border on a regular basis, but they tend to do so for different reasons and go to different places. It is in these neighborhoods that the global meets the local.

Chapultepec is one of the wealthiest neighborhoods in Tijuana. While the typical Tijuana resident earns only about one-fifth as much as a San Diego worker, there are huge differences from place to place and many residents of Chapultepec are quite wealthy even by North American standards. As in most Latin American cities, the best neighborhoods are concentrated near the center of the urban area rather than in remote suburban enclaves and, despite its hybrid nature, this is the case in Tijuana as well. Stereotypically, the Latin elite want to be close to the action or "movement," especially since the countryside does not have the same emotive appeal that it does in Anglo America. The best neighborhoods are located in a linear "spine" that extends southeast from the edge of downtown (Zona Central) to major attractions such as the city's largest golf course and racetrack.[4] Luxurious mansions dot the hillsides with views over the river valley below. Homeownership rates and incomes are high even by U.S. standards and urban services such as water, electricity, and paved streets are ubiquitous. Demographically, the neighborhood appears to be very much like an elite area in San Diego such as La Jolla. This is where many of the older families who have run the city and its economy for years reside.

Chapultepec residents have the best of both worlds. Socially and culturally they have the advantage of living in Mexico and enjoying the traditional political connections of a power elite. They need not worry about being immigrants in a foreign land. Tijuana offers a rich cultural setting with parties, restaurants, and amusements available to all who can afford them. For the things that are not available south of the border, many travel to San Diego on a regular basis.

Wealthy Tijuanans make up about 10–15 percent of the shoppers at San Diego's best malls. Many of the highest quality department stores and luxury shops depend on visitors from Tijuana to be successful. Movie theaters, operas, stage productions, concerts, and restaurants offer products and productions unavailable in Tijuana. Aside from the inconvenience of long lines, crossing the border is easy. Many wealthy Mexicans own houses or condominiums in San Diego (often as a way to get money out of pesos into a dollar economy). There are usually relatives in San Diego as well as the extended cross-border families that are common in elite circles. With legal residence status in the U.S., travel documents (green cards) are always in hand. Important residents of Tijuana are often present at grand openings and political events in San Diego just as San Diegans often appear at similar events in Tijuana.

These "movers and shakers" of Tijuana play an important role as entrepreneurs in the border economy. It would be very difficult for them to play the same roles if the border did not exist or if they did not live in Mexico. Political and social connections are very important in Mexico since, for example, personal contacts with decision makers in Mexico City can be essential when big plans are implemented. Chapultepec provides a lifestyle zone for a unique segment of the population of the greater San Diego/Tijuana region.

The interwoven nature of the economies of the two border cities is epitomized not only by the rich and powerful. Equally complex connections exist in what might be termed the working class in neighborhoods like Libertad. Libertad is an older, established neighborhood dating back to the 1930s. There are many long-term residents who have many family and social connections in San Diego. Residents of Libertad also shop and recreate in San Diego, but not at the same places as their wealthier neighbors. Mexicans account for about three-fourths of the sales in local shops in the border community of San Ysidro, for example. Throughout the largely Latino South Bay area of San Diego, Tijuanans make up anywhere from 20 to 40 percent of the local shoppers. All in all, Mexican consumers spend far more in San Diego than San Diegans spend in Tijuana, despite the emphasis on tourism south of the border. The difference is made up from Mexican commuters working, both legally and illegally, in San Diego and bringing the money home.

Everyone knows that thousands of Mexicans work illegally in San Diego but so far little has been done to stop it. The economy, especially the tourist industry, likely depends on this labor pool to remain competitive. A large percentage of the maids in large

CHAPTER 4

hotels, cooks and dish washers in restaurants, landscapers and maintenance workers, janitors, delivery people, retail sales clerks, and auto repair specialists in San Diego are Latino. Some are long-time San Diego residents, but others are legal or illegal workers from across the line. San Diego is not like cities such as Los Angeles, San Antonio, or New York in the sense of having huge "inner city" barrios. The San Diego/Tijuana region is not only bicultural but binational. Large numbers of workers cross the border each day, while others live part time on one side or the other. Contrary to author Thomas Wolfe's decree, they can "go home again."

San Diego, especially the South Bay area from Barrio Logan to San Ysidro, is full of furniture and upholstery shops, engine repair venues, gardening agencies, and a wide variety of other craft and service operations that rely in part on Mexican labor. The residents of older communities like Libertad are more likely than those of Tijuana's newer peripheral settlements to have economic connections, social and family contacts, and a detailed knowledge of the needs and opportunities on the "otro lado." Indeed, the quality of life of middle-class San Diegans might not be as high as it is without the domestics, gardeners, construction workers, and restaurant workers who find their way into the San Diego economy on a regular basis. Similarly, the quality of life in Libertad would not be very high without the wages these workers bring home. As with Chapultepec, it can be argued that some of the people of Libertad have the best of both worlds; they earn U.S. wages but live in a culturally comfortable setting with much lower living costs than they would have in a barrio north of the border. In addition, even working-class Tijuanans have access to some U.S. amenities. School buses from Tijuana, for example, are a regular feature at the San Diego Zoo.

Politically the border is a fixed and permanent line, but in other ways it is quite fuzzy and malleable. San Ysidro, for exam-

Downtown Tijuana as a tourist attraction for Greater San Diego.

ple, belongs as much to Mexico as to the United States. The population is almost entirely Latino and the businesses, such as Mexican insurance agents and outlet malls, exist primarily to serve people who are crossing the border in one direction or the other. In many ways, it is an extension of Mexico. On the other hand, a large number of people from the U.S. reside in Tijuana and Baja California in order to achieve lifestyles that would be impossible in San Diego. Beachfront cottages and luxury condos that would be unaffordable in San Diego are popular residences in Tijuana. Retirees, especially if they are of Hispanic descent, also find that Tijuana is a good place to live on a fixed income.

Tijuana has many urban problems, but it is a prosperous and dynamic city by Mexican standards. With approximately 4.5 million people, the greater San Diego/Tijuana region is one of the largest agglomerations on an international border anywhere in the world. In a sense, the region is a giant experiment in cross-border cooperation.

LA MESA: AN ALL-AMERICAN
SMALL TOWN

On Thursday evenings during the summer, one of the biggest events in the city of La Mesa takes place on the main street. People bring their old time cars, especially spruced up hot rods from the 1950s, and try to recreate the "cruising" atmosphere of days gone by. Rock and roll bands play on the sidewalk and decent Elvis impersonators are not uncommon. The streets are lively and the cafes are full. On Fridays a farmers' market fills the main street with traditional foods and crafts. For the past thirty years, the city also has hosted an Oktoberfest complete with oom-pah-pah bands and beer tents, an event that attracts visitors from surrounding communities as well as locals. In December, the streets are closed again for an Old Fashioned Christmas Village and Marketplace event with children's rides, carolers, chestnut roasting, and choirs. These types of events are geared toward enhancing the small town feel and community spirit of the town. If *Ozzie and Harriet* or *Leave it to Beaver* had been filmed in San Diego, La Mesa would probably be the setting. La Mesa really is a good, clean, pleasant, and rather average small town but its promoters have tried to create an image that surpasses reality, that of Main Street America.

If La Jolla and Tijuana represent examples of the polar extremes to be found in the San Diego region, La Mesa represents the quintessentially normal. It is very close to average in a number of categories, although the averages sometimes mask differences between neighborhoods. The diversity of La Mesa makes it a refreshing contrast to the overwhelming uniformity of many newer San Diego suburbs. There is a real downtown with lots of traditional "main street" images. There are also older residential streets, apartment districts, hilltop mansions, a suburban mall, a

Downtown La Mesa: a small town "Main Street" atmosphere.

warehouse zone, postwar tract housing, and many other types of landscapes and land uses not found in newer planned unit developments.

La Mesa lies just to the east of San Diego and, as the name suggests, it occupies some relatively high ground between San Diego and El Cajon Valley. It was settled during the late nineteenth century, like many places in East County, as an agricultural center. Around the turn of the twentieth century, scattered farms that concentrated largely on growing citrus crops, especially lemons, occupied the area. The community just to the south of La Mesa is even called Lemon Grove. Things began to concentrate around what is now downtown when the San Diego, Cuyamaca and Eastern Railroad came through in 1889. It wasn't really much of a railroad since it only ran from downtown San Diego into the foothills of East County—about thirty miles. It did, however, help establish a series of small agricultural centers that provided food and later some exports for the little city of San Diego.

La Mesa also benefited from early water projects that led to its being at the end of a flume coming down from the mountains.

Water was a key factor in transforming the barren semi-desert into a lush agricultural region, but supplying it was no easy task. Since rainfall was much more plentiful in the mountains, the trick was to get the water down slope. The San Diego Flume Company was organized in 1886 and began constructing Cuyamaca Reservoir high in the mountains. Using Chinese laborers who had learned to use dynamite and build tunnels while working on railroads, a massive flume was constructed that emptied into the Grossmont Reservoir in La Mesa. This was one of the biggest construction projects in the region, with one of the trestles spanning 1,774 feet. The combination of the two reservoirs, an upstream diverting dam, a twelve-mile natural channel, and the thirty-six mile flume, meant that there was for a time abundant water for agriculture in the La Mesa district.[5]

The project was made possible by the California Legislature's passage of the Wright Act in 1887. Before that time, California used the English system of appropriating water. This involved the use of riparian rights, which assigned control of the water to the persons who owned property along the stream bank or water source. This system worked pretty well in the humid East but not in semi-arid southern California. The Wright Act enabled farmers and communities to form irrigation districts and pool their monies for the purpose of bringing in water from great distances.

There was plenty of optimism, and towns were established all over the area—Spring Valley, Helix, Mount Miguel, La Presa, and more. As often happened in early San Diego, much of this optimism was diminished by a combination of drought and over-speculation. Water began to flow through the flume in February 1889, but by then the great speculative land boom of the 1880s had gone bust. The region turned to the more modest endeavor of profitable agriculture and put town building on the back burner. Even that, however, became problematic when rainfall in the mountains did not materialize.

In 1897, the San Diego Flume Company announced that water would no longer be available for irrigation. A combination of low rainfall, leakage, and increased demand, especially from the growing city of San Diego, meant that there was little water available for farming. The drought continued through 1905 and many East County farmers were forced off the land. The high cost of shipping lemons to eastern markets meant that San Diego could not yet compete with Mediterranean exporters. Water issues eased a little in 1935 when San Diego City and the La Mesa, Lemon Grove, and Spring Valley Irrigation District joined forces to construct a pipeline from the new El Capitan Dam on the San Diego River. A reliable water supply was not assured, at least to the extent that it is assured today, until 1941, when the Colorado River Aqueduct was completed.

In the meantime, a variety of schemes emerged to take up the slack, including bottling what water there was and selling it as a magic elixir (California Waters of Life) and building an immense resort hotel complete with a gondola car on the top of 1,500-foot Mount Miguel. None of these schemes came to fruition. One that did, however, was the hybridization of the avocado from an inedible decorative plant into a highly profitable type of food. By the 1930s, avocados were planted all over the area, and many streets were named after avocado varieties such as Fuerte, Nabal, and Calavo.

The overall decline in population in the area may have actually helped La Mesa. As plans for new towns evaporated along with the water, and as smaller train stations closed, many activities concentrated in what was already the most viable central place. La Mesa City was incorporated in 1912 when it had a total population of 700. Even then it boasted several stores, an opera house, a weekly newspaper, a library, a hotel, and several clubs and lodges. It was also one of the first rural communities in the county to have gas and electric service—a major coup considering the fifteen-mile distance to San Diego. La Mesa's importance increased in 1924 when Grossmont High School, the first in the area, was opened in the northern part of the city.

For the following thirty years or so, La Mesa really was a small town. Although it was connected by rail and highway to San Diego, there was plentiful empty space in between. The reign of agriculture was brief, however, and by the late 1940s and early 1950s the two cities were growing together so that it was increasingly difficult to tell where one stopped and the other started. Motels and drive-in restaurants lined Highway 80 through both San Diego and La Mesa and houses were built ever higher up the slopes of the surrounding hills. In addition, nearly all the rural land around La Mesa in Spring Valley and Lemon Grove was developed during in the 1950s and 1960s. Farms were becoming a thing of the past. The town of La Mesa was being engulfed in a sea of suburban sprawl.

Searching for an Identity: City, Town, or Suburb

Major changes came to La Mesa during the 1960s and 1970s in the form of freeways, malls, suburban sprawl, and urban renewal. By the 1960s, the community had two freeways. Interstate 8 bisected the city, creating a distinctive older south and newer suburban north. In addition, the southern boundary was now the Highway 94 freeway. During the 1980s and 1990s, Highway 125 was completed, making La Mesa one of the most accessible places in the county. With all the cars came pressure for redevelopment. Grossmont Shopping Center opened just to the north of Interstate 8 in the early 1960s and drained some of the life from the nearby downtown, already suffering from a sense of obsolescence and a lack of parking. As a response, during the early 1970s the city opted for an urban renewal plan that obliterated about one third of La Mesa Boulevard, the traditional main street. The new zone featured a strip mall and a mid-rise apartment complex. La Mesa was beginning to look and feel like just another suburb of San Diego.

During the 1980s, the "Two La Mesas" syndrome gained momentum. In the northern half of the city, the shopping center was joined by a variety of big box retailers and specialty outlets. Two major medical complexes expanded and some modest office buildings were put up. Increasing numbers of apartment and condominium complexes joined the tract housing from the 1950s. Southern La Mesa, the older part of the city, went off in a different direction. Here, what remained of the small town feel from the days of yore was identified, preserved, and enhanced. This is the area that epitomizes La Mesa as a distinctive lifestyle zone.

The long defunct train station in the heart of downtown La Mesa was renovated in 1982, and the rail lines have since been converted for use by the San Diego Trolley light rail system. Although the station itself is now visited mostly by railroad buffs, the presence of the original building helps to preserve La Mesa's image as "Main Street, USA." Most of the architecture along nearby La Mesa Boulevard reinforces the small town atmosphere as well. A tall clock tower adds to the sense of time and place while tree-lined streets, storefronts with awnings over the sidewalk, and street-side parking make for a pedestrian-friendly ambience. A flyer from the La Mesa Business Association proclaims: "Cobblestone, tree-lined sidewalks take you back to the small town America of yesteryear."

Although the old downtown or "village" no longer offers the upscale retailing found in shopping malls, there are few gaps in the streetscape. Second-hand book and clothing stores and antique shops abound, with a variety of restaurants and cafes adding to the mix. There are also several more traditional "main street" businesses such as pharmacies, hair salons, dry cleaners, postal outlets, and insurance offices that tend to reinforce the idea that old La Mesa is still the center of town. To a degree, La Mesa Boulevard still represents what geographer Donald Meinig has referred to as the classic Main Street of Middle America.[6] Several highly visible church steeples, warehouses along the tracts, and a courthouse square also give character to the place. In addition, many of the blocks surrounding the downtown contain well cared for older houses and apartments built along traditional tree-lined streets leading into the city center.

La Mesa enthusiastically embraces its image as a classic small town focused on a quintessential main street. In spite of massive redevelopment for shopping malls, freeways, and housing tracts nearby, this image has proven to be remarkably resilient. Topography is an ally in the quest for a vivid sense of place. La Mesa was known as "the Jewel of the Hills" through much of its history, and the city center is surrounded by three substantial hills that give the town center a cozy and well-bounded identity. For at least the past half-century, these hills have been developed as moderately affluent residential neighborhoods giving the downtown a defensive ridge of desirability. In addition, since many of the homes have sweeping views over the center city, there is a greater sense of proprietary interest in protecting it from either hyperdevelopment or decay, which might happen if it were less visible. Although, compared to many other neighborhoods in the San Diego region, La Mesa does have an authentic sense of place, at least some of its identity has been purposefully contrived.

The Image of La Mesa in Real Estate Ads

In any large metropolitan area, real estate agents act as gatekeepers in the sense that they sell not only houses but a neighborhood sense of place to those seeking a change of address. Geographer Brenda Kayzar analyzed real estate advertisements for a variety of San Diego neighborhoods and then interviewed realtors who worked in these areas to uncover what they emphasized in sales pitches to prospective residents.[7] La Mesa, or at least the older southern part, was clearly advertised and sold as an all-American small town with a strong sense of community identity. Written advertisements for houses in central La Mesa often contain key words or descriptors. Often the neighborhood gets as much press as the individual house in the written ads. Phrases such as "Old La Mesa," "walk to La Mesa Village," "heart of Old La Mesa," "historic area," "vintage homes," and "walk to schools and shopping" are quite common. Other terms and phrases include reference to "cozy" neighborhoods with sidewalks and "tree-lined streets." Although access to the entire urban region via freeways and trolley is sometimes touted, it is the term "walking" that stands out as something that sets La Mesa apart from most other suburbs. The words "close" and "near" are often used as well.

Another attribute that is often emphasized is the diversity of the housing stock. Common terms and phrases include "big backyard," "granny flat," "teen's quarters," "RV parking," and "great starter home." Compared to newer and more homogeneous suburbs, La Mesa has a much wider variety of house types, sizes, and price ranges. In this sense, there is some validity to the claim that central La Mesa is a village that could appeal to families, retirees, yuppies, and even extended families. Once again, topography matters. There are million-dollar homes on the tops of the surrounding hills with sweeping views of the town below, as well as modest bungalows closer to the freeways and trolley tracks. At the bottom end of the spectrum, there are pockets of Section Eight (subsidized) housing, mostly in the form of apartment complexes. Between these two extremes there is also great variety, as some homes have been modified and enlarged over the years while others have suffered deferred maintenance. Apartment complexes, retirement homes, condos, and townhouses add to the diversity of housing options. The average price of a house in La Mesa is about the same as for the region as a whole but the wide variety makes describing the "average" house difficult. Interviews with real estate agents not only confirmed but accentuated the importance of the attributes discussed above. In "field trips" around town with local agents, the talk nearly always turned to the idea that La Mesa (or at least Old La Mesa) was a very traditional, all-American town with lots of walkable streets, local businesses, churches, libraries, community spirit, diversity, and identity. The many festivals, street markets, and holiday events were also emphasized. Realtors also emphasized that the area was a place where people felt safe and secure enough to take walks at night and participate in local activities.

To a very real degree, the "Main Street/Americana" image of La Mesa conforms to many of the ideals that advocates of neotraditional urbanism are currently pushing. Features such as houses with "gregarious" facades and front porches built close to tree-lined sidewalks within walking distance of schools, stores, and churches dominate both the neotraditional urbanist literature and real estate ads for La Mesa.[8]

The People of La Mesa

The population of La Mesa is not quite as diverse as its landscape might suggest. In the year 2000 there were 54,749 people in the City of La Mesa, a figure that has remained pretty stable over the past few decades with a 3 percent growth rate between 1990 and 2000. Every part of La Mesa's 9.3-square-mile territory is developed, and so changes in the size and make-up of its population come slowly if at all. Of the total population, approximately 20,000 live in or around what might be called Old La Mesa or the "village." The rest live in a more suburban landscape north of

Interstate 8 or in the hilly fringe of town. Still, the relatively low turnover in the entire community coupled with the "traditional" appeal of the all-American small town image has resulted in a largely white Anglo population. As of the 2000 U.S. Census, about three-fourths of the people of La Mesa claim to be non-Hispanic white, a relatively high percentage for a middle-class community in southern San Diego County. About 13 percent of the population is Hispanic, 4 percent are African-American, and 3 percent Asian. The rest are American Indian, Pacific Islander, or mixed. Minority percentages are surprisingly evenly distributed throughout the city, with only the eastern (elite) hilltop districts having fewer Black and Hispanic residents than the village and the northern suburban fringe.

There is also little evidence of ethnicity in the commercial landscape. The "Mayberry-style" old-fashioned charm that the village encourages does not lend itself (read "allow") much in the way of colorful ethnic signage. The same is true for the major shopping mall (Grossmont) on the northern side of Interstate 8. Ethnic "banner streets" are common in San Diego, but not in La Mesa. One of the "groups" attracted to La Mesa in relatively high numbers is female-headed households. Women are attracted to the La Mesa ambience in the same way that men are attracted to the Lakeside community discussed later in this chapter.

La Mesa is a city of both homeowners and renters. Renters are slightly more numerous, making up about 55 percent of the households—a figure quite comparable to the San Diego region as a whole. Here there is significant geographic variation within the city, with the eastern area on the slopes of Mount Helix having almost no renters while the village area is about two-thirds renters. Not only are most of the apartment complexes either in the village or adjacent to the shopping mall, the smaller bungalows and granny flats tend to be in the older core as well. The percentage of renters may well increase given the high cost of housing and the high level of accessibility associated with La Mesa. A large mid-rise apartment building aimed at the elderly now sits in the heart of the village as part of a transit-oriented development (TOD) project associated with the trolley. Many residents are retired people who have sold houses and moved into a more convenient living situation. Living within a block or two of bridge games at the community center and coffee at the local cafe is part of the La Mesa village mystique.

EASTLAKE: A NEW COMMUNITY PLANNED TO THE LAST DETAIL

Eastlake emphasizes the new and innovative every bit as much as La Mesa emphasizes the old and traditional. The first houses in this vast new master planned community opened in 1986; before that, the entire area was devoid of any type of development. There is little history to divulge since the development sprang to life very quickly with every detail arranged beforehand. It is thus a polar opposite of La Mesa in terms of architectural and temporal diversity. The community of Eastlake is part of the city of Chula Vista, a suburb just to the south of San Diego. Chula Vista itself represents another polar opposite of La Mesa, in that it is large and growing rapidly with new housing projects everywhere. With the help of an aggressive annexation policy, the city has grown to 49 square miles (the same size as San Francisco) with a population in the year 2000 of 173,556. By mid-2002 its population had swelled to 194,000 making it the seventh fastest growing city in the U.S. for the year. Much of its land is still vacant, unlike most other cities in California, and so it could soon become one of the largest cities in the state. In part, this is due to successful projects like Eastlake.

Massive Eastlake construction projects from the air.

New Town Planning and Architectural Uniformity

Architecturally, Eastlake is anything but diverse. It is character-ized by mile after mile of houses alternating among three or four basic models—all beige, two stories tall, with a two-car garage facing the street. A variety of codes, covenants, and restrictions (now common in all large developments in southern California) make it nearly impossible to personalize either individual houses or the streetscape. Everything is aimed at protecting and main-taining the look of the community down to the last mailbox and shrub. The uniformity is magnified by the lack of mature vegeta-tion and so acres, if not square miles, of similar rooftops domi-nate the scene from every vantage point. The fact that the lots are small and the houses are close together makes it seem that the countryside has been "tiled."

The commercial districts and community centers are in the same architectural "style," adding to the appearance of con-trolled uniformity. All this, of course, is acceptable in the name of property values. No property-deflating eyesores are allowed to appear. The bigger the development, the more controls are thought to be necessary since lenders and corporate entities have a huge investment in the place. This represents a major departure from the way neighborhoods were built in the past, especially before the 1950s. "Builders" who purchased a few lots at a time and constructed a variety of different types of houses built older cities. Both profits and risks were small. The infrastructure was the responsibility of the city and so small contractors were able to build what they liked. In huge projects such as Eastlake, the developer is responsible for not only thousands of homes but also commercial centers, schools, parks, and even streets. With millions of dollars involved, nothing is left to chance.

Given the stupendous rise in housing prices over the past few years, there would seem to be little reason for concern about the impact of individualistic and even nonconforming architecture. Still, it is possible that design changes of any kind will be difficult to integrate into the look of the community. When places are initially built to have variety, additional change seems natural, but when homogeneity is the name of the game, individual personalization can look like paste-on decoration.

Finding a Place for Eastlake

Eastlake is located in what not long ago was considered to be a very remote and inaccessible place—rolling foothills about four miles east of downtown Chula Vista. There is little development of any kind nearby and, other than the fine views of mountains and reservoirs, there was little reason to be there. As a result, both highways and amenities had to be built from scratch. Through the 1980s, most new construction in the San Diego region was concentrated in the northern part of the county. Gradually, however, the corridor between Los Angeles and San Diego

An artificial lake forms the core of one Eastlake neighborhood.

became notorious for traffic congestion and hyperdevelopment. With only two freeways linking the two giant metropolises, at least through San Diego County, fierce opposition arose with every announcement of a new housing project that would add to the traffic problem.

After decades of rampant growth, by the 1980s, there were no more areas suitable for megadevelopments in North County. As a result, areas in the southeastern part of the county that are off the beaten track have garnered increased attention. In addition, Chula Vista is one of the few incorporated cities in San Diego County that have been able to annex large tracts of land and facilitate tax-generating projects. It is a city that is not anti-growth. According to population growth forecasts for the year 2020, the Eastlake area will have one of the largest increases in population in the county.[9]

Eastlake is one of several Chula Vista mega-projects. When finished, Eastlake will have 9,000 homes, a business center, and six commercial centers spread over about five square miles

(3,200 acres). The community will also have four parks and six schools to serve its relatively isolated population. Since access to the "life" of the region is not great, Eastlake emphasizes family activities and local, home-centered amenities in its advertisements. Most of the individual neighborhoods are built around themes associated with the great outdoors. In addition to two existing lakes (reservoirs), Upper and Lower Otay Lakes, another lake was built as a theme for one of the neighborhoods. Eastlake Shores includes a beach club, and so long trips to the ocean may not be necessary. Eastlake Country Club and its meandering golf course provide the theme for the Eastlake Greens neighborhood, while Eastlake Trails is next to a wetland preserve. Eastlake Vistas is located next to the largest lake with uninterrupted views of the mountains. The Woods is the most problematic of the theme neighborhoods, since there are few trees anywhere in the area.

Not only is Eastlake relatively remote from most of the major activity nodes in San Diego, although access is rapidly being improved with the construction of new highways, the neighborhoods within Eastlake are not well connected to each other. Each is a separate pod connected to the others by very few through streets. The network of streets epitomizes what has been termed a "loop and lollipop" pattern of curving streets and cul-de-sacs. This pattern tends to reinforce a home-centered lifestyle, since walking to a corner store, or even around the block, is difficult. As a result, automobile travel plays a major role in getting around within Eastlake as well as to and from it. The cul-de-sacs are homogeneously residential while all the commercial activities are located on major parkways.

The street pattern is confusing in that it is far more difficult to envision such a meandering system than a simple grid. Exploration of surrounding neighborhoods, especially for small children, is less likely when getting lost is a real possibility. This too reinforces the ideal of micro-living in a home-centered environment.

The People of Eastlake

At first glance, Eastlake seems to epitomize the extreme in "escape from the city" suburban development in America. In much of the academic and popular literature, such places are usually associated with a relatively homogeneous white population seeking to flee from the diversity of the city. Such is not the case in Eastlake. In this case, architectural conformity tends to mask and perhaps even to facilitate ethnic diversity.

According to the study *Who's Your Neighbor?* published by the Public Policy Institute of California, residential segregation has for the most part decreased dramatically in California over the past decade.[10] There are, however, great differences in this trend from place to place. One of the surprising things to come out of this comprehensive study was that many of the old generalizations about city diversity versus suburban homogeneity have become increasingly inaccurate. Using five categories in the development of a diversity index—non-Hispanic white, Hispanic or Latino, African American, Asian and Pacific Islander, and Native American—it was found that new, fast-growing, middle-class, and often suburban locations are among the most diverse neighborhoods in the state. Conversely, the least diverse were older Hispanic barrios and elite white areas. Thus many central city communities are not diverse since they are often either Hispanic barrios or established, low-turnover white neighborhoods. Examples of such neighborhoods already discussed in this book include Sherman Heights, Kensington, La Jolla, and La Mesa.

Eastlake is ethnically diverse, as is Chula Vista as a whole. According to the 2000 census, the city's 173,556 people include 86,073 Hispanics, 55,042 whites, 7,517 African Americans, 18,410 Asians (often Filipinos), 883 Pacific Islanders, 593 American Indians, and about 5,000 mixed or other. In the older sections of Chula Vista, however, this diversity is often the result of the aggregation of very different types of neighborhoods. For example, some are largely Hispanic while others are largely white.

It is more difficult to examine the figures for Eastlake since census tract boundaries do not match community boundaries, but approximations are possible. For example, in the community of Eastlake Greens, the total population of 7,897 is made up of 3,822 whites, 2,380 Hispanics, 2,383 Asians, 465 African Americans, and 583 "other." The core of the neighborhood is a golf course and there are no separate barrios. These figures hold true in other tracts in and around Eastlake. In most cases, about half the population is white followed by an even mix of Hispanic and Asian. African Americans and Pacific Islanders make up smaller, but still substantial percentages of the total.

Eastlake is not only diverse, but it celebrates this diversity in its advertisements and brochures. Pictures of happy children of all colors frolicking together are common. The sales pitch is that a home in Eastlake is just too good a deal to let prejudice stand in the way of living there.

Diversity, Location, and Design

There are several reasons why diversity seems to work so well in Eastlake. The six most important of these reasons are (1) a location in southeastern San Diego County; (2) a relatively remote location some distance from both established minority and elite white communities; (3) a solidly middle-class character as defined by a narrow range of home prices; (4) an overwhelming majority of homeowners; (5) strict design controls and conformity that not only prevent deferred maintenance but also make "ethnic personalization" in forms like signage and murals impossible; and (6) its newness and the fact that everyone has moved in during the post-civil rights legislation era.

The first reason, a location in southeastern San Diego County, is important primarily because this section of the county has more non-white residents than most others. The potential is there to attract a diverse group of people who do not want to move too far away from friends, relatives, churches, and other social support systems. While at least a few other rural parts of the county have residual reputations as somewhat inhospitable or even racist or "redneck," this is not the case here. It is comfortable for everyone.

On the other hand, its location is far enough way from anything that could possibly be called a barrio or a ghetto that there is no perception of the area as someone else's "turf" or territory or that the community is on the verge of "changing." It is also not part of a rapidly gentrifying elite white community, as are many downtown or beach communities, and so that threat too is minimal. And so the second reason for success is that its diversity is seen as having a real potential to be lasting.

Third, while Eastlake is ethnically diverse, it is not economically diverse. The houses are all in what passes for "middle class" in the overheated San Diego housing market. The vast majority of houses sell from between the mid-$300,000s to the low $500,000s, making them very close to the countywide average. While there are a few lower priced town homes and a slightly more luxurious section, Eastlake lacks the wide spectrum that characterizes many older neighborhoods such as Kensington and La Mesa. There are no mansions or flats over shops. Middle-class values can soften the impact of different cultural landscape tastes. Still, there is pressure to increase the number of housing options. A small section of "luxurious" houses is presently under construction and models are open for inspection. More controversial is a plan to build affordable rental apartments in the community. Over the objections of many residents, the city of Chula Vista recently approved a 150-unit rental complex in Eastlake that it hopes to subsidize through the use of some state funding. The overall range of housing, however, remains relatively narrow.

Not only are most of the houses the same size and price but they are also nearly all owner-occupied. Most of Eastlake hovers around the 80–90 percent owned level with some neighborhoods approaching 100 percent, an extraordinarily high rate for San Diego County. Part of this is due to the lack of apartments, but much of it is due to the "family living" image of the area and its somewhat boring image among renters who could afford to reside there. It is not a "get a rental" neighborhood.

Fifth, and very important and controversial, is the role of strict design controls and architectural homogeneity. It means that "they" (another ethnic group) cannot paint their houses purple, put statues of the Virgin Mary on the lawn, decorate restaurants in gaudy red, or put cars on blocks out front. The banner streets that proclaim ethnic or subcultural identity in cities are rarely permitted in Eastlake. There are also no rainbow flags or political displays. Perhaps diversity is more acceptable in America when it can have no impact on the landscape (read property values).

Finally, since everyone in Eastlake and the communities nearby has moved there recently, there are no vestiges of segregation and racial steering by real estate agents. Most residents arrived during the 1990s and may even be too young (or foreign) to know that such policies once existed.[11] In addition, since the community is new and occupied almost entirely by young families, there hasn't been time for the area to develop a wide range of life-stage communities such as elderly and college student districts.

It may be that California's and San Diego's tremendous and increasing diversity itself works in favor of more integrated communities. Instead of the "us and them" attitudes found in many areas where there are only two major groups, such as black and white in much of the South or white and Hispanic in parts of the

Southwest, San Diego has a much better balance. There is often no majority and therefore no minority population. With four or five common ethnic groups and quite a bit of mixing, it is often difficult to decide who is what, especially in an otherwise homogeneous landscape.

LAKESIDE: DELIBERATE DISORDER IN A LIBERTARIAN SUBURB

Although Lakeside is located in a suburban ring about the same distance from downtown San Diego as Eastlake, the two communities could not be more different. They represent two ends of the suburban spectrum in population, landscape, and lifestyle. The character and even charm of Lakeside comes from disorder rather than order. It is neither incorporated nor part of a planned development. In one sense, it is not a place at all but rather a state of mind. Consequently, it is relatively difficult to come up with data for Lakeside since it essentially has no official boundaries. The name encompasses several disparate and often poorly connected neighborhoods. A roadside sign gives the population of Lakeside as about 40,000 but the consensus core probably includes only half that number. In addition, much of the Lakeside ambience spills over into a huge, largely rural census tract with about 2,000 inhabitants. While precise numbers for Lakeside are hard to assemble, it is easy to describe its basic landscape and sense of place.

Lakeside tends to attract people who find phrases like "down home country living" appealing. While more a stereotype than a reality, Lakeside is often associated with ranches, trucks, and Country and Western music. It is overwhelmingly non-Hispanic White and "minorities" sometimes associate it with cowboy culture and rednecks. Three of the five census tracts that I use to

The suburb of Lakeside emphasizes its role as a location for horse ranches and other forms of recreation close to mountains.

define Lakeside had no Blacks in the year 2000 and one had no Asians. It is, however, far more culturally diverse than such images suggest. Joan Embrey, for example, who has appeared on national television as an ambassador for the San Diego Zoo, has a ranch containing interesting and exotic animals in Lakeside and many Zoo-related events have been held there. Still, this tends to confirm the ranch and country ambience.

There are four themes that can be used to describe Lakeside as a different and unusual type of San Diego community: libertarian suburb; Old West; ranch and horse country; and rural recreation gateway. Each theme is reinforced by Lakeside's traditional, if diminishing, remoteness and its location in a physical cul-de-sac ringed by mountains and reservoirs. The fact that the area is unincorporated and relatively unplanned reinforces the theme of rural freedom versus municipal regulations. The landscape exudes self-conscious rusticity as well as freewheeling disorder.

Libertarian Suburb

Much of Lakeside conforms to what has been described by Robert Barnett as a "libertarian suburb."[12] Nearly all the restrictions so carefully articulated in the codes and covenants of most planned developments such as Eastlake are not only absent here but they are also vigorously and aggressively opposed. The landscape of nonconformity seems to call out for bumper stickers that say, "They're not going to make me do that." The core of old Lakeside includes a wide variety of building types, piles of materials, empty lots, random trucks and trailers, dusty streets with no sidewalks, and colorful signs. The residential areas close by exude individualism even though most of the houses were originally part of typical middle-class tracts.

The diversity of landscapes in Lakeside is more purposeful than historical. While many of the older neighborhoods of San Diego have a variety of building types, resulting from their coming of age before World War II when builders constructed a few houses at a time and residential and commercial activities were more integrated, in Lakeside even homogeneous landscapes have been personalized. Many houses feature additions and embellishments that would not be acceptable in planned communities and the yards are often filled with trucks, trailers, and machinery. Such landscapes have often been categorized as lower class or even poor, when they appear on the fringes of eastern cities, but this is not really the case in Lakeside. While it is not known as an upscale community, most of the houses are substantial and million-dollar mansions are beginning to appear on the ridges above town. Still, the area is quite mixed, with ancient shacks, boxy apartment complexes built during the 1950s, and substantial suburban homes built in the 1960s and 1970s, all sharing space with a tire yard. What appears at first glance to be excessive clutter, however, is the result not so much of poverty as of a spirited "wild west" individualism.

Houses and businesses use a variety of colors, themes, fences, vegetation, add-ons, flags, porches, basketball hoops, and other embellishments to celebrate nonconformity. No one needs to worry about property values in San Diego County. There is a market for laissez-faire neighborhoods and they are increasingly hard to find in the planned unit developments of Southern California. The relatively affordable houses in central Lakeside have attracted a young population and lots of families. Homeowners dominate most neighborhoods, although the situation is reversed near the business district where nearly all the apartment complexes are found. It is also one of the few remaining close-in communities that still have a large number of mobile home parks.

Old West

The center of Lakeside's commercial district is an official historic district complete with guidelines, if not overly strict controls. The theme is the "Old West," with signs saying "Hay Feed" and "Saloon" dominating the signage on the main street. Some buildings have pictures of cowboys and horses painted on the sides. There is also an old wooden church along with some small cottages in the district that are less "western" but fit in just the same. Proposals to make the theme more pronounced with Disneyfied embellishments such as hitching posts were defeated, and so the place has a reasonably authentic feel.

The Old West theme fits in well with the trucks, motorbikes, and piles of materials associated with the libertarian suburb theme in that the latter reinforces a sort of New West/Old West merger. The cowboy still rides, but on newer stuff. The fact that Lakeside is not far from several large Indian reservations also reinforces the western theme.[13]

The cowboy theme associated with Lakeside may act as a deterrent to at least some minorities seeking a residence in this relatively affordable community. While many Latinos find the cowboy motif reasonably comfortable, Blacks and Asians often have a tougher time identifying with the western ambience. This is especially true since the western theme is not just a paste-on aesthetic but is reinforced by real economic activities, especially ranches.

Ranch and Horse Country

Lakeside is nestled in a series of narrow valleys surrounded by steep slopes and rocky mountains. As a result, many of the roads leading out of town are dead ends; they go up a valley and stop. This is horse country. The combination of a ranching tradition and the inaccessibility of the narrow canyons for suburban development has helped keep the real cowboys in business. The fact that large earthen dams on the San Diego River and other streams sit above some of the valleys may also dissuade some potential developers. Of course, these days many of the ranches serve as riding stables for an urban clientele, and city folks often board their horses in Lakeside. If anything, this enhances the exotic western ambience as establishments compete for customers.

The landscape of ranches, horses, hay, corrals, horse trailers, and wooden "ranch house" signage has an impact on the local sense of place far beyond the actual number of people involved in the business. It is not uncommon to see people in cowboy hats and boots riding along the side of the road. The valleys around Lakeside are some of the few places left in the San Diego metropolitan area where horses can be seen running through authentically rustic territory.

Rural Recreation Gateway

Lakeside is now and always has been a place to go for rural recreation. The name evolved from the Lakeside Inn, established in the 1880s at the end of a rail line from San Diego. The Inn attracted hunters, fishermen, and explorers to the wild country where the rugged mountains met the more civilized foothills. The combination of steep mountains, a location along the San Diego River, and lots of ranches has brought city folks out for a day of fun for over a century. A small pond called Lindo Lake was the focus early on for everything from picnics to auto racing. As new reservoirs were built, Lakeside became more literally true to its name as boaters and fishermen flocked to the area. Today, Lake Jennings, San Vicente Reservoir, and El Capitan Reservoir lie just above the community and feature parks and marinas. It helps that Lakeside is often hot and sunny when coastal San Diego is cool and foggy. Swimmers thus have a climatic option.

Much of the land beyond Lakeside is off limits to development: it is controlled by such entities as the U.S. Forest Service, Bureau of Land Management, city parks or reservoirs, and water and sanitation districts; serves as a wildlife sanctuary run by the Audubon Society; or is part of several large Indian reservations. Only the latter are experiencing growth and development as Indian casinos attract investment. But more about that in the next chapter. Being surrounded by lands in these categories along with steep and rocky hillsides, generally makes Lakeside a permanent frontier for standard suburban development.

The recreational opportunities associated with the Lakeside physical environment are evident in many of its residential landscapes. A drive down nearly any street leads to views of campers, boats, trailers, tents, fishing equipment, mountain bikes, and assorted weekend fun paraphernalia. The visibility of such accouterments conflates with the theme of libertarian suburb since it is unlikely that the clutter of recreation would be allowed in a planned unit development. Freedom of expression and freedom to store toys go hand in hand. The prevalence of large yards and mini-ranches makes for even more storage space than might be expected in a place like Eastlake where lots are small. Similarly, the opportunity to sell recreational equipment is greater in the ad hoc commercial landscape of Lakeside than in the standard suburban malls of newer developments.

LIFE ON THE FRINGE OF URBAN SAN DIEGO

As in the previous chapter, I have here tried to emphasize the diversity of lifestyle zones that are not simply a matter of social class and ethnicity. Because the international boundary (Tijuana) and extreme differences in wealth (La Jolla versus most other places), social class and political context are important variables. Still, the concept of lifestyle zones plays a role. While a potential home seeker might well be able to afford to locate in La Mesa, Eastlake, or Lakeside, and commute to work and shops with similar ease or difficulty, it is likely that lifestyle and landscape image will inform the choice. For wealthy Latinos, it is possible that La Jolla and Tijuana may both be appealing but for very different reasons. Culture, politics, economics, and landscape preferences can lead to a much more complicated decision-making process than many classic models of city structure suggest.

Just as central San Diego provides a wide variety of lifestyle zones that are based as much on self-image and leisure activities as on income, race, and occupation, so too do the immediate suburbs of the city. In the next chapter, we will see that this theme continues to be important in the more remote reaches of the metropolitan area.

CHAPTER FIVE

Communities Beyond the Fringe

All the previously discussed communities are in the continuously built up or "urbanized" part of San Diego County. Although they were shaped in part by enthusiasm for creating particular types of physical and cultural settings, they were also subject to the typical pressures that we associate with all large metropolitan areas, whether urban or suburban. In other words, all of the communities, possibly excepting Tijuana, comprise what is considered the contiguous greater San Diego metropolitan area. The next five communities to be discussed are different in that, while they are a part of San Diego County and thus the official metropolitan area, they are physically and historically separate from the core city. They are, to a much greater extent, unique places in their own right. They are only gradually and begrudgingly admitting to being part of urban San Diego.

The southeastern quarter of San Diego County is dominated by the city of San Diego. While the physical gradient from coast to mesas, mountains and deserts exists, to some degree it is hidden by the shear mass of the urban landscape. Such is not the case in the northern part of the county, although given current rates of growth, that eventuality may emerge. Rather, in the north, there is no dominant city, no core holding the disparate parts together. As the oft-quoted Gertrude Stein is supposed to have

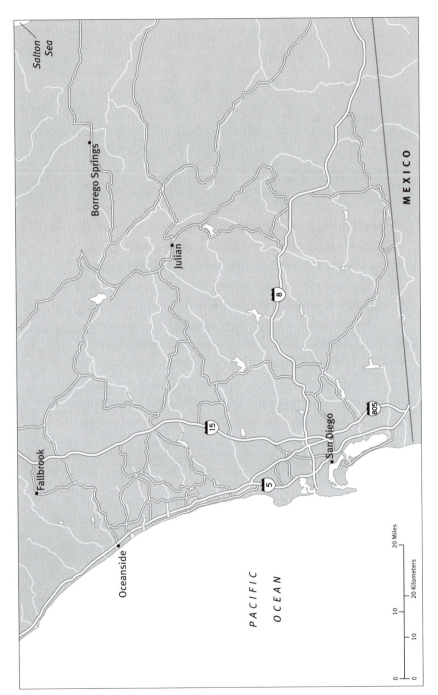

Communities beyond the fringe.

said, "there is no there, there," at least in the sense of a consensus identity. There are, however, many small and scattered identities and each one competes for its share of the limelight.

In the North and East County communities I discuss in this chapter, the physical settings play a critical role. In some cases, the physical environment is by far the dominant reason d'etre for the community's very existence. As always, however, it is usually the recognition and exaggeration of a physical attribute that really defines the community sense of place, since the local "culture" often grows out of attempts at place commodification. As in many urban neighborhoods, "nature" here is debatable because imported vegetation and policies such as the suppression of forest fires create a somewhat artificial natural environment. In addition, the lack of well-developed infrastructure often makes the physical setting seem more important, because basic services such as a reliable water supply and monitoring of coyote and mountain lion populations are not always present.

Let me repeat—the places discussed in this chapter really could not be more different. They are the Barona Indian Reservation, the old gold-mining mountain town of Julian, the desert retirement community of Borrego Springs, the bucolic "almost wine country" village of Fallbrook, and the beachfront and military-dominated town of Oceanside. With the possible exception of the Barona Reservation (which is primarily shaped by its unique cultural and political context), these communities are heavily influenced by their locations in four distinctive physical realms. These realms occupy four parallel north-south running bands starting along the coast and continuing to the mountains and desert: coastal plain (Oceanside), interior valleys (Fallbrook and Barona), mountains (Julian), and desert (Borrego Springs).

These places are not part of the contiguous urbanized region but rather sell themselves as unique settings within the Greater San Diego area. Many of the people who live in them celebrate the physical identities of the places with daily activities such as surfing, hiking, rock climbing, gardening, boating, dirt biking, and the like. These are not "normal" bedroom communities, but they are increasingly part of the "commuter-shed" for employment in the county's more traditional urban centers. They also function as major attractions and tourist destinations for the metropolitan population. The question on the minds of many residents is "How long can we keep from being engulfed in the urban tide?"

THE BARONA INDIAN RESERVATION

San Diego County has eighteen Indian reservations and seventeen tribal governments, more than any other county in the United States and more than many regions of the country. Currently, these reservations occupy 125,000 acres of land, approximately 4 percent of the county.[1] Until quite recently they were notable primarily for their high rates of poverty and unemployment. Their landscapes were associated with ragged pastures, unkempt cottages, and decrepit trucks. All this has changed drastically in recent years with the rise of Indian casinos and all-purpose megaresorts. While similar resorts have blossomed throughout the U.S., they have become major players in shaping the San Diego region due to sheer numbers, access to the large local and tourist populations in southern California, and scarcity of prime developable land in the county. In addition, other issues, such as battles over water, make Indian land use decisions very important in San Diego.

Throughout the United States, as in San Diego County, federal policy toward Indians (this is what they call themselves here—not Native Americans) has swung back and forth between isolation on reservations and relocation for assimilation, at least for the past century. It is beyond the scope of this brief section to recount the plight of Indians in North America or even to go very deeply into the history of Indians in San Diego County. Still, I will try to explain a bit about how and why this region has so many reservations, as well as where they are located.

Indians in San Diego County

Before the coming of Europeans to San Diego, the region was one of the most densely settled parts of what was to become the U.S. The area offered a rich variety of foods even in the absence of agriculture and may have supported a population of over 50,000. Most of the Indians were migratory—they had no large, permanent settlements and moved seasonally between the mountains and the sea in search of food and the other necessities of life. Villages, when they existed, were usually found along rivers or estuaries where food was plentiful.

The arrival of the Spanish decimated the Indian populations. Still, Indians made up about three-fourths of the county population as late as 1850, even though the combination of disease, extermination, and the introduction of vast cattle ranches had reduced the Indian population to about 5,000 people by the early years of the nineteenth century. In addition, high rates of intermarriage made it increasingly difficult to determine just who was a Native American. A very high percentage of the Spanish/Mexican population became "mestizo" or mixed early on.

During the eighteenth and early nineteenth centuries, the Spanish made every attempt to force the native population to reside on agricultural lands run by the missions. Called *reducciones*, these were intended to concentrate the Indian population in areas where they could be controlled and converted. "Wild" Indians in the countryside were not to be tolerated. By 1820, over 4,000 Indians resided at the two major missions—San Diego in the south and San Luis Rey in the north. They were often treated as little better than slaves, and runaways were hunted down. The Mexican government secularized the already declining missions in 1833 and many Indians moved elsewhere, taking advantage of the growing demand for their labor.

By the time California became a state in 1850, Indians often provided cheap labor for industries along the waterfront and in construction. Perhaps the biggest source of employment, however, remained the ranches. With training from the mission days, many Indians worked as vaqueros and so, ironically, Indians were often cowboys.

The number, variety, distribution, occupations, and migratory customs of the native population in San Diego made for some complex compromises when reservations were first established in the county in 1875 (after a brief first attempt in 1870). Over the years, land has been added, subtracted, and rearranged, leading to a patchwork of small reservations throughout the county. Much the same occurred throughout the U.S., with Indians holding 155 million acres in 1881 but only 77 million by 1900. As in most of the country, Anglo-Americans took the best lands for towns, farms, mines, and ranches. The Indians got what was left over and consequently, had a hard time surviving. This was especially true under the old rules, as tribes could not obtain bank loans for economic development without relinquishing sovereignty. Some Indians literally starved, while others drifted away to cities or sought work on farms and ranches.

San Diego lacked well-known tribes such as the Cherokee or Apache, and there is some confusion about what exactly constituted a "tribe" versus a language group or "band" or subgroup. Still, the consensus is that San Diego County includes four Indian groups, the Kumeyaay, Luisenos, Cupenos, and Cahuillas. In addition, Indians from many other tribes have migrated to San Diego over the decades from places such as Oklahoma and North Carolina, complicating the ethnic identity issue. My focus here is on the Barona Reservation, one of the places associated with the Kumeyaay group.

Indian Gaming Casinos

Indian reservations are no longer associated with poverty and deprivation in San Diego County. Indian gaming has become big business all across the country, but nowhere is this truer than in San Diego County. State laws vary and local authorities often have had different interpretations of what is legal. Throughout the 1980s, bingo games and small card rooms became sources of revenue for California Indians, especially in the growing absence of federal support.[2] Throughout the 1980s, local governments in California (as elsewhere) raided Indian gaming parlors and often arrested participants while confiscating cash.

The U.S. Supreme Court ruled in 1987 that states have limited authority over Indian gaming, and in 1988 Congress passed the Indian Gaming Regulatory Act, which essentially paved the way for its expansion. The concept of Indian sovereignty was enhanced as tribes were given the right to establish all three classes of gambling venues, from social clubs (class 1) to bingo halls and card rooms (class 2) to casinos and horse tracks (class 3). Tribes that wanted to have class 3 venues, however, were required to have Tribal-State Compacts that spelled out the details of who would be responsible for what. In California, most of these compacts were finalized in 1999. The National Indian Gaming Association was set up to monitor and defend tribal activities as conditions vary from state to state.

Gaming at Barona

As the city of San Diego started growing in the 1850s, a group of Indians living in what is now the Mission Valley area were relocated to a remote valley along the upper reaches of the San Diego River known (by the Spanish) as Capitan Grande. The area became an official reservation in 1875. Two bands of Kumeyaay shared the valley until 1931, when everyone living in the Capitan Grande Reservation was forced to move because the city of San Diego bought the valley to create a reservoir. The two Indian groups used the money from the sale to buy new land. The Los Conejos group purchased the Barona Long Ranch, now known as Viejas. The Capitan band bought 6,385 acres of land on the Barona Ranch and began resettling in 1932. Gradually, both groups took on the name of their reservations, as in "the Barona Indians." The two groups still share control of the remaining 15,000-acre but uninhabited Capitan Grande Reservation.

Gaming began on a small scale in Barona with bingo halls in the 1980s, and by the early 1990s larger facilities and growing advertising budgets began to lure eager gamblers to the reservations. The boom really started in the late 1990s when the Tribal-State Compact was signed, paving the way for massive new developments. The Barona Valley Ranch Resort and Casino opened in 2002 and quickly became a major tourist destination for the region. Today, Barona has one of the biggest and most impressive casino complexes in California. The 283-acre site includes a 300,000-square-foot casino, a first-class golf course, and a huge (397-room, eight-story) hotel-spa with some luxury suites going for more than $400 a night. Restaurants, stores, a gas station, a fitness center, tennis courts, a business center, off-track betting, a racetrack, a 2,000-space parking garage, a wedding chapel, and a venue for major concerts are also included in the complex. Barona has become a major destination, at least for southern California. A frequent shuttle service connects the San Diego suburb of El Cajon to the casino.

Certainly, the local economic picture has changed. The casino employs nearly 3,000 people and has, it claims, eliminated unemployment on the reservation (once as high as 70 percent). New

Casino and hotel on the Barona Indian Reservation.

luxury houses are springing up along dirt roads and fancy SUVs have largely replaced old pick-up trucks in the driveways. At present, there are 453 enrolled members of the Barona Tribe who are eligible for a share of the revenue. Approximately 500 people live on the reservation, of whom 350 are tribal members, but that will probably change as the boom continues. The numbers involved in the cultural revival will be interesting to follow, since the county has eighteen reservations and a total of 15,300 people (2000 census) who identify themselves as Indian only. Of these, 5,873 are "enrolled" tribal members. Of course, far more people have some "Indian blood" and it may well be that the combination of prosperity and pride will encourage more ethnically mixed people to identify with their Indian heritage. Several hundred acres of Barona have been set aside for future home sites for tribal members.

Reinventing a Culture and a Lifestyle

Keeping Indian culture alive during decades of poverty and discrimination was a tough job. In the eyes of many, to be an Indian was to be a loser. Funds for cultural activities and classes were scarce to nonexistent. All this has changed with the success of the resorts and casinos. The Barona Reservation features the Barona Cultural Center and Museum, with a wide variety of exhibits and events aimed at revitalizing, reinventing, and diffusing several aspects of the traditional Indian way of life.

The museum contains over 2,000 artifacts from the region, including pottery, coiled baskets, grinding stones, tools, rock art, and pipes. Traditional houses and kitchens have been reconstructed in order to actively demonstrate traditional activities. Special exhibits include photographs of the reservation over time, often with special themes such as Indians as cowboys and ranchers. The cultural center also sponsors a variety of special luncheons and speakers aimed at not only tribal members but also casino workers and the general public.

There are language classes offered by both professional teachers and old-timers who remember the local words and sayings. Elderly tribal members have a forum for telling stories from their childhoods on the reservation. The Center also funds the Barona Indian Charter School with classes for children in grades K-12. Classes in language, history, arts, science, and contemporary Indian life are helping establish a new enthusiasm for and pride in the Indian way of life. The complex includes a library, a computer center, a tutoring office, and a Head Start Program. Field trips to the San Diego Zoo and Wild Animal Park are organized around themes such as "Animals of the Ancestors." Other field excursions demonstrate ways to collect willows and other materials for the construction of traditional dwellings.[3] Professors from local universities and community colleges offer courses on the reservation dealing with topics such as "California Indian Culture and History." One community college even offers a Cross-Cultural Studies Indian Gaming Degree. The tribe provides $15,000 scholarships for those wishing to attend college.

Many events are held off the reservation, such as special arts festivals in Old Town San Diego or Pow Wows at various locations throughout the county. The goal is usually the same—to demonstrate that Indian culture is alive and well in San Diego. The tribe publishes a regular newsletter that keeps track of the growing list of activities.

The profits from the casino and resort are making it possible to create a kind of place-based community that does not conform well to the normal city and suburban definition of metropolitan area. But in San Diego County tribal lands are increasingly leading the way in the exurban boom. This is especially true for reservations that are relatively close to major population centers or along major highways. The Viejas group, for example, has a major casino and factory outlet mall a few miles out of town on Interstate 8, the major freeway leading east to Arizona. Both Barona and Viejas serve as major entertainment venues with regularly scheduled big name concerts at relatively low prices. They are following the Las Vegas model as closely as possible and only time will tell if giant teepees, pueblos, and hogans will someday compete in scale and glitz with New York/New York.

Indian Resorts: Is the Sky the Limit?

Casinos are springing up all over San Diego County, but no one knows how many can be sustained in the long run. San Diego has more Indian gaming facilities than any other county in the state. Three tribes had casinos before the Tribal-State Compacts were signed in 1999, and since then five more have been added. Altogether, fifteen San Diego tribes have signed compacts, and plans are afoot for new projects on all but two of the reservations. In addition, there is activity just over the county line in Riverside, where in 2002 the Pechanga Tribe opened the largest facility in the state, complete with a fourteen-story hotel, concert venue and convention center. There is concern that the tribes are beginning to compete with each other and that the market will soon become saturated, especially with over forty Indian casinos elsewhere in California. Even with California's current limit of 2,000 slot machines per tribe, the opportunities for gambling are mushrooming. If competition intensifies, the larger, better-located casinos may still thrive, but marginal operations could see tough times despite the revenue sharing among the tribal casinos that is in effect. Are the tribes putting all their eggs in one precarious basket?

Many have suggested that efforts at economic development should become more diverse and that office and industrial parks could be constructed once the expensive infrastructure needed for large resorts is in place. The better educational and health facilities that have been financed by gaming should also make tribal members more competitive in the job market.

Indian Gaming and Environmental Issues

Barona is located only about six miles north of Lakeside on a winding, two-lane highway. The traffic it generates has created significant consternation in that once sleepy community since nearly everyone heading to Barona passes through one tiny intersection. Similar concerns exist throughout the county. If all the casino plans are brought to fruition, the urbanized region of San Diego could be ringed by hyperdevelopment with little or no "countryside" left between the city and the higher mountains. Country roads would be continually jammed. However, the most immediate major concern about the scale and pace of development on Indian reservations revolves around the ever-present concern of water. The issue is especially acute in Barona.

Reservation projects are not subject to the same regulations and controls the county requires in other areas. Nevertheless, the tribes generally try to cooperate with other agencies in estimating the environmental impacts of major development. In the spring of 2000, the Barona Indian Band issued an "environmental evaluation" for the creation of five lakes associated with its proposed golf course and casino. The semi-arid valley is nearly 100 percent dependent on the groundwater underlying the reservation and the surrounding community. The Band estimated that there were 7.3 billion gallons of water stored in the groundwater basin, but neighbors and local government officials were skeptical of the claim. There was fear that Barona's proposed massive pumping of up to 500,000 gallons of water per day just to irrigate the golf course would endanger the wells in the surrounding rural communities, most of which also rely entirely on groundwater.

When the huge Indian wells were completed in 2001 and started pumping, the wells of the twenty families living just south of the reservation began to dry up. The tribe maintained through 2002 that it had access to a separate and abundant aquifer and was not responsible for nearby problems. The argument folded when it was discovered that Barona was secretly trucking water in during the night just to satisfy its own demand. The tribe then suggested that its emergency situation merited an exemption from the California Environmental Quality Act to allow it to pipe millions of gallons of untreated Colorado River water from Lake San Vicente into its aquifer. The water would be used primarily for the golf course, but it would also flow into neighboring wells and mix with formerly potable supplies. The tribe would build its own water treatment plant, but that would not help the people nearby. The battle still rages and Barona's neighbors claim that their property values have suffered.

The issues are complex and involve not only the type and scale of appropriate development in the back country (there are many non-Indian golf courses in other parts of San Diego County), but also the degree of sovereignty the tribes should have when it comes to public policy issues like clean water, clean air, and public health. If they are indeed sovereign, then hyperdevelopment in San Diego's rural fringe will be a source of great controversy for the foreseeable future.

High Profile Politics

Barona and the other Indian casinos not only sponsor and fund a wide variety of activities on the reservation, they increasingly are major players in the political and cultural life of the greater San Diego region. Billboards with celebrities such as singer Kenny (the Gambler) Rogers urging people to visit Barona appear frequently throughout San Diego. The tribes, who now go almost exclusively by their reservation/casino names rather than traditional ones like Kumeyaay or Luiseno, sponsor concerts, sporting events, and charities of all kinds. Between 1994 and 2001, Barona's total contribution to San Diego charities, including sponsorships, was over 4.6 million dollars and the amount is increasing annually.

The tribes have also become politically powerful. In lieu of local taxes, the reservations agree to pay fees to local authorities that at least theoretically cover the costs of transit planning, highway patrols, and the like. Of course, politicians may get contributions from the tribes as well, based on their willingness to lend a sympathetic ear. There is some concern that San Diego's Indians have become too powerful and may be stretching sovereignty to the limit. One recent example is the attempt by the Native American Heritage Commission to stop development on land that is considered sacred to a tribe even though it is outside any reservation. Since sacredness is a hard thing to evaluate, this issue could easily become hotly contested. The exurban ring of reservations around San Diego is indeed an interesting place.

In the California recall election of 2003, Republican challengers charged that Indians were not paying their fair share and had worked out favorable deals with the Democratic incumbent. Just after the recall succeeded, a firestorm swept through San Diego County, burning much of the reservation and many homes but not the golf course-surrounded casino. San Diego's tribal governments have offered significant funds for the reconstruction of the back country well beyond the reservation, and so the political context for the continued success of the Indian cultural revival in San Diego keeps changing.

THE OLD MINING TOWN OF JULIAN

Julian is located in the Cuyamaca Mountains about sixty miles northeast of downtown San Diego, but it considers itself a completely separate world. The town of Julian contrasts nicely with Barona. As a mining boomtown during the 1870s, it helped precipitate the idea of Indian reservations, since miners, loggers, and others were rapidly invading even the mountain retreats of the already displaced indigenous population. The conflict continues to this day, notably recent tribal efforts to keep a gold mine from opening in nearby Imperial County on what they consider to be a sacred site. Julian also represents another extreme in physical setting and environmental challenges. While water is always an issue in San Diego, the Julian area's biggest problem is the ever-present danger of fire. Some would argue that it is simply not a very good place for wise people to live, but many do, and once again much of the attraction has to do with the invention and selling of a powerful sense of place.

Julian advertises itself as "San Diego's premier mountain retreat." The mountain ranges of San Diego, unlike those in the Los Angeles area, are not really very high, with only a few peaks reaching 6,000 feet. The town is located in a former meadow at 4,225 feet (considerably lower than Denver), so the mountain retreat idea may be a stretch. Still, it is one of the town's three important sources of imagery, along with historic mining town and cute village.

The Boom of the 1870s

Julian, named after Mike Julian, who settled in the valley in 1869, began in earnest a year later, when many men whose lives were disrupted by the Civil War drifted west and ended up searching for gold just about everywhere in California. Fred Coleman, who had worked the Mother Lode in northern California, spotted some yellow flecks while watering his horse in a small creek on the slopes of Volcan Mountain. And so it was that the San Diego area began to experience a mini-gold rush. The boom, while intense, was short-lived. At its peak in the mid-1870s, Julian had about 600 residents, but by 1876 most of the mines were closed and interest waned. New discoveries brought a brief revival in 1887 and there was a period of relative prosperity during the 1890s and early 1900s. By 1910, however, all the mines were closed, and no major activity has taken place since that time, although some "recreational" mining began in the 1970s when the price of gold soared. Indeed, the possibility of finding gold looms large in the image of the region.

The limited success of gold mining in Julian was largely due to the nature of the veins or, more precisely, the lack thereof. The gold-bearing quartz in the Julian area was extremely localized and difficult to work. Where substantial veins existed at all, they tended to be horizontal and subject to cave-ins. As a result, it was difficult to get adequate financing for a major operation. At the time, California banks were concentrated in San Francisco, where gold mining expertise was common. Banks were leery of the questionable situation in the mountains of San Diego. San Diego's miners also had to do without the considerable expertise in engineering and geology that existed farther north. In addition, transportation was a problem, since there were no railroads, navigable rivers, or decent roads in the area.

The total amount of gold mined in San Diego was not impressive. Altogether, approximately 5.2 million dollars worth of the precious metal has come out of the local mountains. The Stonewall Mine, the single biggest operation in Julian, produced about 2 million dollars worth. While northern California attracted 100,000 prospectors and created a long string of mining towns along what is now Route 49, San Diego was left with just one, Julian.

History plays an important part of the Julian image. The entire village has been a historic district since the 1970s and many nonconforming land uses, such a 1960s-era gas station, have been removed during recent years. Where possible, there has been a careful recreation of the northern California "mining town" look. Historic Days, sponsored by the Julian Chamber of Commerce, is an annual event, and official historic sites are plentiful. Major historic attractions include the old jail, Julian Town Hall, the Pioneer Museum, Pioneer Cemetery, and a variety of Pioneer and Victorian era houses. There are horse-drawn carriages, gold mine tours, quilting competitions, craft shows, and walking tours of the historic area.

The Cute Village

The second theme that attracts both residents and visitors to Julian is that of a cute village. The actual historic town of Julian is only about three blocks long with both sides of the streets lined with candle shops, curio stores, cafes, and bed and breakfast inns. Although there are many places in San Diego County from La Jolla to La Mesa that call themselves villages, all are much larger and more developed than Julian. Julian really is a village, and it really is cute. Strict architectural and sign controls regulate a somewhat irregular if not disheveled western mountain town to create a rather interesting landscape.

With the demise of gold mining, new themes emerged both to support the area economically and, later, to attract tourists. Chief among these were apple orchards. While apples may not be very exotic in most parts of the U.S., they do not grow well in lowland San Diego. Apples, apple trees, apple pies, and a sort of All-American apple pie way of life seem worth a visit to San Diegans who are tired of oranges and bougainvillea. Apple festivals and famous venues selling apple pies and other treats help enhance the rural, agricultural flavor of the village. Apple Days, the major festival, was established in 1949 and it is estimated that more than 10,000 apple pies per week are baked and sold in Julian in October, as visitors from all around southern California converge for a colorful and filling frontier experience.[4]

The village also offers wine tasting, cozy cottages, art galleries, used book stores, and other usual elements, creating a village ambience that tends to work pretty well. During Apple Days and other festivals, Julian can become extremely crowded, with cars parked along the highway for a mile around. This is especially true during autumn weekends when many people come to look at what passes for fall colors in San Diego.

Most of the residents of the greater Julian area do not actually live in the village. Approximately 300 people live in the historic core, about half the number who lived there a century ago, while another 4,000 or so live in nearby residential areas. The biggest neighborhood is the Pines, a large cluster of suburban style houses on narrow, winding roads just outside town. Most of the houses are on the hills and are surrounded by forests. Without the trees the developments might look like standard suburban projects, but with them they are considered mountain retreats.

Although the mining town theme is oft repeated, the residential areas around Julian are anything but rough and ready. Most have substantial homes with wooden decks, on two or three acres of land. According to recent advertisements, they are valued at only slightly less than many close-in suburban neighborhoods, despite the relative lack of services and infrastructure. Julian is a white, middle-class place with many $300,000 houses. Problems can arise, however, when too many people live in the woods.

A Place in the Mountains

When it comes to attracting permanent residents and visitors alike, neither gold nor apples can compete with Julian's mountain ambience. It is located between two major peaks, Volcan Mountain and Cuyamaca, just north of large and heavily visited Cuyamaca State Park. People associate Julian with hiking trails, dirt biking, rock climbing, and horseback riding in a mountain environment. Tourists often come to Julian as part of a day of recreating in the mountain parks. Julian is, above all, a mountain town.

Its most attractive feature, however, is also its most problematic. High mountains can catch significant amounts of rainfall and have a permanent snow pack, but the mountains of San Diego County are not that high. Consequently, drought conditions are not uncommon. The highest peaks may get over 35 inches of rain in a good year, but Julian itself usually receives about 24 inches. Snow is rare and does not last more than a day or so. Summer temperatures in the San Diego mountains are actually higher than along the coast and sunshine is the norm. Things can get very dry.

The vegetation profile typical of the local mountains is chaparral up to about 3,000 feet, oak parkland between 3,000 and about 4,500 feet, oak forest between 4,500 and 6,000 feet, and pine forest above 6,000 feet. At upper elevations the most common trees include Ponderosa pines, Jeffrey pines, Coulter pines, sugar pines, and incense cedars. Photographs from the 1890s show that the natural landscape was oak parkland, that is, a relatively open, grassy meadow with scattered oaks. Although the area had probably been denuded of some trees for mining operations by the 1880s, most of the lumber came from the higher pine forests and there was a noticeable lack of stumps in and around Julian. While some of this land has since been converted to ranches and orchards, forest growth has also been encouraged, and that has sometimes become a problem.

In the popular imagery, mountain resorts should be forested, especially when associated with cozy log cabins, fireplaces, hiking trails, fall colors, and, of course, apple pies. People who want to live in the mountains usually want to live in the woods. For varied reasons, the forests around Julian are dangerously overgrown. The main contributors are policies emphasizing fire prevention rather than the historically normal pattern of recurring fires; the development of "forest communities" where residents plant (especially pine) trees to create a desired mountain ambience; recurring drought conditions; and the increasing menace of bark beetles that attack and eventually kill vulnerable trees. Due to these factors, the forests around Julian are too dense, too old, too sick, too dry, and perhaps at too low an elevation. There is also far too much undergrowth and dead wood at ground level.

It has been estimated that there are approximately ten times as many trees per acre in these forests than should exist under ideal conditions. In addition, because many areas have been protected from fire for a long time, most of the trees are over fifty years old, including short-lived varieties that rarely live longer than that. By some accounts, about half the trees could be classified as dead or dying. There is great variety from place to place and species to species, of course, but the problem is widespread. As the trees become unhealthy due to competition for water and age, they have become increasingly vulnerable to attacks from several species of bark beetles.

The Threat of Fire

Fire in San Diego's back country is a very serious problem. In September 1970, more than 180,000 acres (about 265 square miles) burned when a fire started on the western slopes of Cuyamaca Peak and headed west toward the suburbs of San Diego. For days, the sky rained soot and ashes and people stood on their suburban rooftops with hose in hand. When fires of that magnitude happen today, the damage is far greater, since so many more people live in vulnerable areas. There have been many other serious fires in the county over the years. The recent fires that have most affected the village occurred in 2002, when the Pines Fire devastated 66,000 acres and destroyed 40 homes, and in 2003, when the Cedar Fire burned nearly 400,000 acres and destroyed several hundred homes in the Julian area. Both fires came close to obliterating the historic village of Julian and only yeoman efforts by firefighters using trucks, planes, and bulldozers kept them at bay. In the end, only houses in the nearby forested residential areas were burned. Given the situation in the mountains of San Diego County today, it seems that future disasters are inevitable.

Many of San Diego's forests are artificial creations that have resulted from significant human intervention in normal cycles of growth and change. Some additional kinds of intervention, such as controlled burns, are needed now, but a consensus is hard to achieve. San Diego's forests have little commercial value, in part because of the types of trees, especially in their current condition. There could be a market for firewood, although that market could become saturated with extensive clearing. Opening the area to logging is thus not a particularly viable option. The National For-

The historic mining town of Julian is a cute mountain retreat for San Diegans, but it is often threatened by fire.

est Service could carry out planned forest clearing within the boundaries of the Cleveland National Forest, but budgets are tight. In Julian, however, the issue involves a collision between lifestyle and safety.

While Julian is warm in summer, winter evenings can be cool or even cold and the (rarely) snowy mountain retreat in the forest idea has a powerful appeal. Using different approaches to landscaping the areas around houses is bound to be controversial. Grass lawns are not feasible and desert-like xerophytic vegetation does not fit with the image of a mountain town. Nevertheless, new images of the ideal lifestyle may be needed if expensive, dangerous, and deadly firefighting episodes are to be avoided in the future.

What is a mountain town and what does it look like? What are the factors involved in making one sustainable both culturally and environmentally? Fire is the major but not the only threat to the idealized Julian way of life. Others involve possible overdevelopment, crowding and traffic, high housing costs, the elimination of service workers, and even potential problems associated with the cohabitation of children, household pets, and predators such as mountain lions. Julian is not an incorporated town and so comprehensive planning for the area is difficult.

BORREGO SPRINGS

When people think of San Diego they usually think of a place with an ideal climate—never too hot or too cold. This climate exists, however, only in about two-thirds of the county. East of the mountains, a very different climatic regime prevails. The low desert of eastern San Diego County is one of the hottest places in the U.S., with the average high temperature in July hovering around 107 degrees Fahrenheit. Occasional temperatures of 125 degrees are not uncommon. The Sonora Desert is in the rain shadow of the Peninsular Range Mountains and almost devoid of any influence from the cool ocean currents offshore. Precipitation varies widely, from zero in some years to five inches in one month when late

Mountain houses destroyed by the Cedar Fire in October 2003.

summer tropical storms come up from Mexico. The yearly average of just under seven inches is not that different from coastal San Diego, but the distribution and reliability are. The region's only reasonably consistent water supply comes from mountain runoff in the form of springs. The San Diego portion of the Sonora Desert is on the western fringe of the Imperial Valley. Until 1907, San Diego County extended all the way to the Colorado River and included the entire valley, including the newly created (1905) Salton Sea. With the establishment of Imperial County, San Diego was left with what seemed to be a relatively useless corner of a potentially irrigable region. A series of canals brought Colorado River water into the largely below sea level valley during the early decades of the twentieth century. Indeed, the Imperial Valley with its rich harvests of winter crops has become a very different kind of place from the original desert. Water battles still rage, with urban San Diego competing with Imperial Valley agriculture for access to the Colorado River. Towns like El Centro and Calexico give Imperial County a population of about 150,000, but the major metropolis of the region is Mexicali, Mexico, a border city with perhaps 1.5 million people. The desert, therefore, is far from uninhabitable, although some San Diegans might think otherwise.

Anza-Borrego Desert State Park

The first recorded visits by Europeans to what is now eastern San Diego County occurred in 1772, when Spanish soldiers from the San Diego Presidio entered the area in search of deserters. In 1774, Juan Bautiste De Anza, looking for a good overland route from Sonora, Mexico, camped at a Cahuilla Indian Village and noted a reliable spring that he named San Gregorio. It later gave rise to Borrego Springs but it took a very long time. The area was ignored for more than a century.[5]

Anza-Borrego Desert State Park is an attraction for those who want to live in a desert environment.

A few cattlemen arrived in the late 1870s, but it was not until around 1910 that the first non-Indian settlers began to homestead the Borrego Valley. The first successful well was dug in 1926, leading to the establishment of some irrigation farming. The small settlement of Borrego Springs included a post office, a small grocery store, and a gas station. It was still, however, in the middle of nowhere with few roads over the mountains or even to the agricultural communities to the east. There was little reason to go to Borrego Springs. All this began to change with the establishment of Anza-Borrego State Park in the early 1930s.

During the late 1920s, a few naturalists began to recognize that the desert portions of San Diego County are exceptionally interesting and scenic. With elevations ranging from over 6,000 feet to below sea level, there are a variety of ecological zones in close proximity. The canyons, springs, and occasional palm groves support a wide variety of wildlife, including bighorn sheep. Magnificent displays of wildflowers appear in early spring along with desert cacti and ocotillo. Geological phenomena such as Fonts Point provide glimpses into Pleistocene sediments. The desert is also a major archaeological site. A wide variety of Indian artifacts including metates and morteros for grinding seeds, cairns or trail markers, middens, and pottery shards still remain. In addition, there are petroglyphs and pictographs painted or etched on rock walls. As the value of these things came to be recognized, efforts to protect this special environment gained momentum.

In 1927, the state legislature created the California State Park Commission, and in 1928 plans were submitted for a state park in the San Diego desert. The first land was acquired from the federal government in 1933 and a state park custodian was appointed. The park was greatly enlarged in 1941 with the acquisition of land south of Highway 78, and the first campground was constructed in 1949. In 1957, what had been Borrego State Park and Anza Desert State Park were consolidated to create what is now the largest state park in the entire United States. Over the years, more facilities were constructed culminating in a large visitor center completed in 1979.

Anza-Borrego Desert State Park is huge, more than 600,000 acres, about 940 square miles. It stretches nearly sixty miles north-south and twenty-five miles east-west. It includes seven distinctive geologic and geographic regions, each with its own character and personality. Right in the middle sits the unincorporated town of Borrego Springs. Since the settlement predated the establishment of the park, town and farm owners, although few in number, managed to exclude it from the protected zone. The park has given the small community an identity and a reason to exist.

Borrego Springs as a Desert Resort

The small settlement of Borrego Springs has struggled for a long time. During World War II, both the Army and the Navy had a presence in the area and brought paved roads, electricity, and an airstrip. For the first time, there was at least a minimal infrastructure. After the war, optimism ran high that the area could be developed into a resort modeled after Palm Springs. Access was still a problem, though, with no major pass through the mountains similar to the one in the Los Angeles-Palm Springs area. The fact that the park surrounded the community was a problem as well as an asset, in that it was hard to get approval for highway programs through the protected zone. Still, developers appeared and aggressive advertising campaigns featuring celebrities and politicians were engaged to sell the area as a premier winter resort.

In the 1950s, the De Anza Country Club was established complete with a golf course and 300 home sites. The Borrego Air Ranch, a small central mall, and a condominium project were completed during the 1960s, but the community remained pretty sleepy. The fact that it was competing, to some extent, with efforts to create a similar resort at Salton City along the shores of the Salton Sea made things more difficult. The desert resort market in California was limited during the immediate postwar decades. Some growth occurred in the 1980s, after the visitor center was opened three miles from "downtown," as tourists now had a focused destination to head for in the vast and sprawling park. In 1998, the Borrego Valley Inn opened as an upscale retreat with at least some of the amenities associated with Palm Springs. The current permanent population of Borrego Springs is just under 3,000, with another 10,000 residing there during the winter months when the midday temperatures hover around 70 degrees. Without the glitz of Palm Springs, visitors and winter residents are more likely to be interested in the natural attractions of a relatively pristine desert environment, interspersed with an occasional round of golf or tennis and a dip in the pool.

Borrego Springs as Exurban San Diego

Over the past decade, Las Vegas has been the fastest-growing metropolitan area in the United States and Phoenix has not been far behind. Much of this growth has been overflow from California. As housing prices and the costs of doing business have skyrocketed in cities like San Diego, both people and companies have moved eastward to the desert, where land is relatively flat and cheap. Some of this overflow growth has gone to the greater Palm Springs/Indio area in Riverside County's Coachella Valley as well as the Imperial Valley. Could some of this growth end up in Borrego Springs simply because there are fewer and fewer options?

So far, Borrego Springs has not experienced anything approaching explosive growth, but according to projections by the San Diego Association of Governments the area could gain significant numbers of jobs and people by 2020.[6] The area excluded from the park contains about 65 square miles of relatively flat, easily developed land. Water supplies now used for irrigated agriculture and ranching could be diverted to residential and commercial areas. There is land zoned for both heavy and light industry, and as the Palm Springs area, North San Diego County, and Imperial County grow, Borrego Springs is becoming at least a little less remote even without new highways.

So far, Borrego Springs has sold itself as a winter resort and a gateway to the nation's largest state park. It pushes its grapefruit festival, desert wildflower season, and a variety of carnivals, pageants, car shows, and tennis tournaments. Most of these activities are very climate specific, taking place in the middle of the San Diego "winter." The threshold population and buying power needed to sustain a viable city are largely lacking during the summer months, and Borrego empties. This does not happen in Phoenix or Las Vegas, and so it is possible for life to go on there. A new image of year-round, relatively inexpensive living and working in a beautiful if rugged environment will likely evolve as even desert space is coveted for development.

FALLBROOK

Metropolitan San Diego is different from most urban areas in that there is no easy escape to a relatively bucolic agricultural landscape. To the west the Pacific Ocean and to the south the international border and Tijuana block the way. To the east, although some imagery associated with ranching and orchards still exists, the mountains and deserts provide the dominant landscape theme. Only to the north is there any remaining semblance of large-scale agriculture. The emphasis is on flowers, avocados, tomatoes, and citrus crops, with wineries providing a new source of imagery and amusement. The problem, however, is that this is the main corridor between Los Angeles and San Diego and the biggest crop, of late, is housing.

The North County Corridor

For over four hours on the afternoon of August 20, 2003, a suicidal man, waving a gun while sitting in a disabled vehicle, led police to close all lanes of the incredibly busy Interstate 15 during the height of rush hour traffic. Cars and trucks were backed up for many miles, and while some of the traffic could be rerouted to the equally overloaded Interstate 5, there were few other options. These two freeways, along with a winding coast road for part of the way, are the only highways between two of America's largest urban areas. Lanes are being added all the time, but already the highways look like vast parking lots at some junctures.

Closing the highways causes tremendous chaos and it is not a rare event. In May 2003, a construction site accident at the I-5/

805 merge just north of La Jolla turned the commute from North County into a half-day experience. In July 1999, another pistol-waving lunatic parked in the middle of a freeway for several hours and seemed to be going for a record traffic jam. Major fires also closed I-15 in autumn 2003. Still, the vast majority of growth in San Diego over the past few decades has been on the coastal plain and nearby rolling countryside of the North County Corridor, especially along the already overloaded I-15, ten to twenty miles inland from the beach.

There are three major reasons for the North County boom, two of them quite obvious. First, a location between Los Angeles and San Diego is clearly optimal for various kinds of businesses seeking access to markets, transportation facilities, a large and diverse labor shed, and new facilities in a suburban setting. Second, land and housing costs are relatively low, at least inland from the coast, and people seeking a suburban dream house are willing to commute both north and south for vast distances along I-15 to find an affordable option. These options are most likely to exist in Riverside County and the extreme northern fringe of San Diego County. Housing tracts are appearing everywhere.

The third reason for the boom is less obvious and fits into our quest for understanding the relationship between the physical environment and place making. The region around the San Diego/Riverside County line provides the closest thing to an idyllic agricultural landscape that metropolitan San Diego has to offer. I refer to the area as Fallbrook, since that community is in San Diego County, but I include Temecula in Riverside County in the discussion since it is both a main housing overflow zone and home to the major players in the local wine industry.

A Bucolic Landscape

Fallbrook is located several miles away from busy I-15, but close enough to be an accessible place for those who need to get away from the urban world. It is adjacent to the eastern boundary of Camp Pendleton Marine Base, but it is a considerable distance from the main camp headquarters, and so is not usually thought of as a major gateway. Bucolic is the main theme in housing ads for Fallbrook. Perhaps the most common terms used in describing the community are "country" and "countryside," and one of its strongest selling points, according to the ads, is the size of the available lots. Rather than emphasize the characteristics of the individual houses, ads focus on the characteristics and size of the acreage. Related to this, is an emphasis on what you can do with the lots if you live in a setting like Fallbrook. Terms such as "park-like acreage," "just bring horses," "home with income from lemon grove," or "walk under canopied oaks" are typical.[7]

Much of the land in and around Fallbrook has been zoned for large lots (one to eight acres) or agriculture (more than eight acres), so housing tracts, though they exist, are not common. The infrastructure of Fallbrook does not extend very far, so large lots are required for septic tanks and leach lines. Still, gated communities and speculative housing are gradually intruding on attempts to preserve a country lifestyle; they are an escape from both the city and the suburbs.

Unlike the situation in much of East County, the land around Fallbrook is not rugged and untamed. It is neither the mountains nor the Wild West; it is "countryside." The gentle landscape lends itself to "strolling around picking fruit off the trees" and driving along winding country lanes. The area even boasts the "last free-flowing river in southern California."[8] The implied imagery of landed estates is sometimes carried through with references to architecture. When styles are mentioned, they often use words like "chateau." While the theme is rural, the actual toil involved in living on a farm is rarely mentioned. Even the Fallbrook tourist industry is in on the theme. It published "Agricultural Points of Interest in the Fallbrook Area," listing rural stands and other

Idyllic agricultural landscapes near the community of Fallbrook.

places where fresh produce and flowers can be purchased and a little country atmosphere soaked up. The town also celebrates a Farmer's Festival.

Agriculture accounts for nearly 20 percent of the local economy, and Color Spot Nurseries, Inc., the nation's largest supplier of bedding plants, is the single largest employer. There are more than fifty nurseries in the area along with a few vineyards. Avocado packing plants also add to the agriculture industry employment base.

Many aspects of the Fallbrook image have remained constant for a long time, especially the idea of panoramic views of the countryside, large lots, and privacy. Other themes, however, have changed dramatically. Twenty-five years ago, Fallbrook frequently made the news as the home of San Diego's Ku Klux Klan leader. The relatively isolated (protected), white community was located well away from the major social changes that occurred in the 1960s and 1970s. Today, the area is better known as a burgeoning artist colony. As artists have been forced out of the lofts and central neighborhoods of San Diego, many have come north to reflect on nature and paint scenes of avocado trees and picturesque farmscapes. Other changes involve the emergence of the area as an incubator for new high-tech firms making such things as medical devices and software. A 200-acre industrial park has been created to foster these industries but is small compared to the 28 square miles zoned for agriculture.

The combination of small roads and large lot zoning will probably mean that the area will experience relatively modest increases in population over the next decade or so. On the other hand, the 2000 population of the unincorporated "village" of Fallbrook was more than 37,000, up from 22,000 in 1990, which makes it one of the fasted growing areas in the county. According to the census, 8,509 households are homeowners while 4,359 are renters. Despite the bucolic estate imagery, renters are a necessary part of an agricultural labor force. Hispanics are also necessary. Although the area is still overwhelmingly non-Hispanic white by California standards, about 75 percent in the five core tracts, most of the rest of the population are Latino. Very few blacks or Asians have found happy valley but Spanish is widely spoken. The density of the 56-square-mile area is low, but not as low as advertisements might suggest, and it may be a struggle to keep the crowds at bay.

Drawing the Metropolitan Line

So far, the biggest crowds have bypassed Fallbrook and headed across the county line to Temecula. Temecula with its sixteen wineries reinforces the theme of idyllic rural landscapes. Billed as having a perfect climate for vineyards, comparable to that of Napa-Sonoma in northern California, Temecula features wine tasting tours, bed and breakfast inns, and a variety of events aimed at rural-seeking tourists.[9]

Temecula has become a major overflow region for San Diegans seeking (slightly) more affordable housing. Since Temecula is part of the existing Riverside/San Bernardino Metropolitan Area, it will never be considered part of San Diego. It is, however, only about twenty miles from major North County growth centers such as Vista and Escondido, and San Diegans are flocking in. The city of Temecula had 2,700 people in 1970, but by 2003 it had passed the 75,000 mark and is expected to reach 100,000 by 2010. The vast majority of its web sites are real estate ads. Houses sell for about $100,000 less than comparable dwellings in San Diego, and the area is beginning to offer amenities as well as flat, developable land. An "Old Town" was largely rebuilt (invented?) in 1998, and shopping malls, hot air balloon rides, and a variety of festivals now complement the wineries as major attractions. Housing tracks spill over the hillsides above the vineyards and so the sense of place that now exists may not last for long.

Like Tijuana to the south, Temecula is increasingly related to the San Diego region, functionally if not officially. The inability to "annex" adjacent fast-growing places is a major reason the San Diego Metropolitan Area is growing more slowly than many others such as Atlanta or Dallas-Fort Worth.

OCEANSIDE

The city of Oceanside, on the coast 35 miles north of downtown San Diego, has had many identities over the years, and new ones are emerging all the time. For the past few decades, it has been most associated with the huge Camp Pendleton Marine Base next door. Its other identities include the home of a major Spanish mission settlement, an early beach resort, and, most recently, a centrally located place for new types of industries and businesses.

Not far from downtown Oceanside is Mission San Luis Rey de

Francia. During the late eighteenth and early nineteenth centuries, it was the major settlement in North San Diego County, competing only with San Diego in the south. Consequently, the area served as a hearth for early agriculture and roadways in what is now San Diego County. It also was a major center for huge Mexican land grants once the missions were secularized. The mission (1798) and the nearby Rancho Guajome Adobe (1852) provide considerable historical interest for the local tourist industry.[10]

With the coming of the railroad and American settlers during the 1880s, the town of Oceanside was established at the beach to provide recreational opportunities for the already existing North County population. By 1888, the population of the newly incorporated city exceeded 1,000 and a bank and newspaper were established. A long pier, the first of six, was built into the ocean and by the 1890s the community had three hotels. The resort dimension has continued and Oceanside now has a harbor and 800-boat marina, the only one north of Mission Bay in central San Diego, as well more than three miles of beaches. During the 1960s, the city pushed the now politically and dermatologically incorrect slogan "tan your hide in Oceanside."

Camp Pendleton

The main thing that sets Oceanside apart from the many other San Diego County beach communities is its location as the gateway to Camp Pendleton Marine Base. Pendleton occupies the far northwestern corner of San Diego County and is America's largest Marine Corps base. Its eighteen-mile length along the coast serves as a greenbelt between the sprawl of greater Los Angeles/Orange County and San Diego. Without Camp Pendleton, there is the distinct possibility that some of San Diego's identity would be lost in a vaguely defined greater southern California metropolis. As it is, most of the coastal section of the base is devoid of

Oceanside Harbor is the only marina between Mission Bay and Orange County.

any kind of development except a Highway Patrol border checkpoint.

Except for lack of access to the public, Pendleton serves as a sort of giant military theme park for those stuck in traffic along Interstate 5. Tanks, planes, and boats often perform exercises within the vast expanses of the base. Despite the occasional explosions, it is also a kind of nature preserve with over 400 species of birds and animals, including 14 on the endangered species list. Oceanside, the first town to the south of this vast open space, thus serves as the gateway not only to Camp Pendleton but also to San Diego County. The worlds north and south of Pendleton are quite different.

Camp Pendleton was established in 1942, and its impact on the city of Oceanside was immediate and dramatic. Oceanside had a population of 4,652 in 1940, but by 1950 it had mushroomed to 12,888, swelling to 18,000 by 1952, with the start of the Korean War. The demand for housing and municipal services exceeded the supply, as Oceanside became a military beach resort.[11]

Camp Pendleton occupies 125,000 acres or approximately 200 square miles of land. The fact that this amount of land could be assembled so quickly along the California coast goes back to the former Mexican land grants. A grant of 133,441 acres was made to Pio Pico and his brother Andreas in 1841 and they established the Rancho Margarita and Los Flores. The rancho changed hands several times over the decades but it was basically still intact in 1942. At that time, the heirs of James Flood and Richard O'Neill, wealthy San Franciscans who had purchased the property in the 1880s, sold the land to the Navy for $4.2 million.

Today, Camp Pendleton is a city unto itself with a daily population or "workforce" of about 55,000. There are nearly 6,700 family housing units on the base, but many people live off base. There are hospitals, schools, day care centers, sewage treatment plants, restaurants, golf course, bowling alley, fire stations, and seven gas stations for the nearly 70,000 vehicles registered on the base. Still, many of the activities the 35,000 Marines and 3,500 Navy personnel seek are in Oceanside. This has caused some "town-gown" problems over the years similar to those found near large universities. When vast numbers of young people hit the bars and beaches of Oceanside on Saturday night, the place can be quite lively.

Diversifying Oceanside

The problem with being so closely associated with Camp Pendleton is that the economy can fluctuate wildly with the comings and goings of the Marines. During the Gulf War and most recently with the war in Iraq, large numbers of Marines have been shipped out for long tours of duty. When this happens, local businesses can suffer, especially during the winter months when tourism is down. Newspaper accounts of empty cafes and stores appear regularly, featuring especially those with a solidly military clientele. After years of dependence on the uneven rewards of military and beach resort revenues, Oceanside has now increased its efforts at economic diversification.

The population is already diverse. Oceanside is one of the few communities in coastal North County with a high percentage of minorities. Approximately 54 percent of the population classify themselves as white, while 6 percent are black (just under the county average), 30 percent Hispanic, 5 percent Asian, and most of the remaining 5 percent American Indian, Hawaiian, or other. It is the only part of North County with a significant, nearly 10,000 strong, black community. Oceanside is thus more like many of the South County communities than the rest of the "far north." Obviously, Camp Pendleton is the major factor. The nine tracts closest to the base are even more diverse with large concentrations of blacks, Hispanics, and Filipinos. Its large military and ethnically diverse population sets Oceanside apart from other San Diego beach towns and gives it a distinctive identity that is less elite than most other north county beach cities.

Oceanside anchors the western end of a major population center in North County. The city itself has over 161,000 people residing in its 42 square miles, making it the third largest city in the county. Oceanside, unlike most beach cities, has grown inland for some distance, following the boundary of Camp Pendleton. Together with the nearby cities of Carlsbad, Vista, San Marcos, and Escondido, it represents a contiguous urban agglomeration of over half a million people. This agglomeration, located along state highway 78, represents the major population center in the county apart from the city of San Diego. In population and economic structure, Oceanside has become far more diverse than its popular image might suggest.

A new slogan for the city is that it is the "center of southern California." Roughly midway between downtown San Diego and the major Orange County node of Anaheim/Costa Mesa, Oceanside is right in the middle of a complex and growing region. Relying in part on relatively low land costs and taxes and in part on a large market and labor force, Oceanside has become a significant commercial and industrial center. Sporting and recreational equipment are manufactured in the city along with biotech and medtech products. Will Oceanside's identity and personality be obliterated by all this growth and sprawl or will the combination of beachfront, harbor, and 35,000 Marines protect it?

THE REST OF SAN DIEGO COUNTY

I have tried to show in the fifteen case study communities examined in the last three chapters that metropolitan San Diego has a large number of very different types of places that do not easily conform to the old city and suburb stereotypes. Most of these places are the result of people settling in widely varying physical environments and then trying to accentuate those differences in physical setting by creating and selling a place identity. Of course, cultural and economic differences play roles as well but even holding those factors constant, the mountain, beach, valley, and mesa towns of San Diego offer very different kinds of lifestyle zones. When variables such as military bases, international borders, and Indian political autonomy are thrown in, the differences become even more extreme. Does everyone in San Diego County live in such placeful communities? I hesitate to make a judgment.

At first glance it would appear that a great many San Diego neighborhoods are quintessentially "normal" in that they look very much like city, suburban, or rural settings anywhere in the United States. Closer examination, however, demonstrates that many of these average places have identities that may not stand out like those in, say, Little Italy or Julian, but nevertheless are highly valued by residents. In other cases, I suspect that there is relatively little community cohesion or sense of place, physical, cultural, or otherwise. I do not, however, intend to name those communities. I will let the readers of this book make their own judgments.

THINKING ABOUT METROPOLITAN AREAS

In Chapter 3 I discussed some new ways of thinking about the spatial structure and organization of our sprawling American metropolitan areas. Perhaps the best way to conclude is to suggest that many if not most of the communities embedded in our urban regions are made up of a combination of "reality" and "wishful thinking" or myths. Reality might encompass such things as land costs and uses, population make-up and density, income and education levels, and transportation flows. The myths involve the ways in which people see, or in some cases would like to see, their communities. This is not really new, since most metropolitan residents have tended to seek neighborhoods that would enhance their idealized images of social class. That is what the selling of suburbia was all about. Today, however, especially in a physically diverse region like San Diego, the opportunities for whimsy and place making have increased in number. As discussed earlier, it is possible for middle-class San Diegans to live in areas that allow them to be (or pretend to be) surfers, prospectors, wine-makers, ranchers, dazzling urbanites, or Spanish hacienda owners.

Perhaps the best way to think about urban areas is to map and model the realities and then to overlay those representations with a grid of more whimsical characteristics. Kevin Lynch and others have attempted to map the way people perceive their environments but the current situation involves more than perceptions.[12] Residents now are more likely to have the money, education, and motivation to try to transform their landscapes into a kind of theme district that reinforces their senses of identity. A variety of architectural controls, ethnic organizations, semi-economic hobbies, and theme commercial ventures can be used to create very different types of places from surfer strips to quaint mountain villages. A major concern is that rising housing costs will lead to a diminished middle class, with a proliferation of sterile gated estates for the rich and struggling housing tracts for a growing lower middle class. So far, however, there is so much invested in housing by those who live in the diverse neighborhoods of San Diego that the quest for place will likely go on for some time.

San Diego may not be typical in this regard, but neither is it unique. All across America, metropolitan areas are expanding to include formerly rural communities, resorts, and even mining towns. As these places join the postmodern world of display and consumption they may well be revitalized as theme districts for new residential and commercial areas. From the Inner Harbor in Baltimore to Nob Hill in San Francisco, new kinds of places are being created and old ones refurbished. It is both fun and interesting to watch it happen.

Epilogue: Planning in "America's Finest City"

Although the preceding chapters have focused on how people turn spaces into places through a combination of ideology and lived experience, the topic of urban planning in a more formal sense is not irrelevant. This is especially true since San Diego has been the setting for some well-documented battles over growth management and environmental quality. Over the past three decades, a variety of individuals and groups have questioned the overall planning context for the region and have suggested that disaster is just around the corner unless there are significant changes in policy and procedures. The century-year-old contest between smokestacks (growth) and geraniums (environmental quality) has never really died down.

The major issue in all of this is the rate of growth itself. The San Diego region, many argue, simply has too many people, especially since it sits between Los Angeles to the north and Tijuana to the south. But there is no realistic way to limit growth in American cities. Even China and the Soviet Union found it nearly impossible to eliminate migration to major cities. Growth, therefore, is not really the issue. San Diego's population will continue to grow and there is precious little that can be done to stop it. Even outrageous housing costs and egregious traffic congestion do not dissuade people from coming. The real issue is growth management. Can growth be accommodated without sacrificing environmental quality? Can San Diego be planned so as to retain its character and sense of place and avoid becoming another Los Angeles? Can San Diego be designed so that it continues to look and feel like a special place? The jury is still out.

Surprisingly little has been written about San Diego in the urban academic world. In addition, that which exists often presents conflicting evaluations of trends and policies. Two of the most recent examples of such varying perceptions of the situation include Richard Hogan's book *The Failure of Planning: Permitting Sprawl in San Diego's Suburbs, 1970–1999*, and Gene Bunnell's section on San Diego in his book *Making Places Special: Stories of Real Places Made Better by Planning*.[1]

Hogan's book is highly critical of planning in San Diego and argues that the region has been destroyed by greed, sprawl, and congestion. The author takes a critical, often Marxist, approach and condemns developers and politicians for working together as part of "republican capitalism." While there are some very good points buried in the book, it is extremely difficult to evaluate the specifics since the author has chosen not to name any of the real communities or contacts he learned from. All the case studies as well as the interviewees have made-up names, so Hogan's criticisms are tough to verify.

Bunnell takes a much more positive stance with regard to planning in San Diego. His long and detailed chapter on the city is entitled "A Hundred-Year Planning Legacy (Periodically Interrupted)." While he is critical of some events and policies, Bunnell generally argues that San Diego has a long history of reasonably successful planning. He also names his interviewees and uses the correct names of the communities he examines and so is easy to critique.

As in most cities, over the years San Diego planners have done many things that have turned out to be both wise and unwise in hindsight. Some of the worst policies were those that allowed sprawling development in places like Mira Mesa to the north and

Otay Mesa to the south long before there were adequate services or transit linkages. Other bad decisions include encouraging chaotic and uncoordinated development in Mission Valley long before there were any attempts at flood control or environmental preservation. There are too many examples of bad planning to mention in detail, but certainly the 30-year delay of the completion of Interstate 15 through City Heights, placing a huge Naval Hospital in Balboa Park, and encouraging the random construction of (ugly) "dingbat" apartment complexes in older neighborhoods should be mentioned. Of course, not all of these decisions were made by San Diego itself. The federal (Naval Hospital) and state (I-15) governments often were often primarily responsible for bad planning decisions.

On the other hand, there have been a great many planning successes in San Diego during the postwar period. Chief among these have been the revitalization of downtown, including thousands of units of housing, a new convention center, a baseball park, waterfront promenades, the Gaslamp Quarter Historic District, and Horton Plaza shopping center. Downtown has gone from one of the dullest and dreariest downtowns in America to one of the liveliest in just two decades. Other notable successes include the creation of Mission Bay Park, a comprehensive light rail transit system, the "natural" flood control channel in Mission Valley (and the subsequent rezoning of the area to include a mix of commerce and housing), various in-fill projects such as the Uptown Project in Hillcrest, and the creation of an urban village complete with new schools and housing in City Heights. Once again, city planning alone was not responsible for all of these successes but some leadership was involved. In the downtown area, the Centre City Development Corporation, a public-private partnership, directed much of the growth and change.

The problem of assigning blame and credit for what has gone on in the city brings us to an important issue, the power (and lack thereof) of planners in particular contexts. The situation has been especially problematic in California over the past twenty-five years. Given the constraints that have been imposed over this period, San Diego has been lucky to have any planning at all. Just as the first really comprehensive land use plan was published in 1979, the effects of 1978's Proposition 13 came home to roost. "Prop 13" was a statewide tax revolt that turned back property tax assessments to 1975 levels and limited subsequent assessments to 1 percent of market value. Immediately, monies flowing into local government coffers were cut by half and most cities have never caught up. In order to get by, cities have had to rely on state government, most often in the form of kickbacks from sales taxes. Consequently, every political entity has competed for strip malls and shopping centers since residential property cannot pay its own way. In addition, developers have had to charge a variety of fees for schools and parks thus driving up the cost of new (and eventually all) housing. As long as state surpluses were available, things held together, but by the early 2000s, everything began to collapse. With the state budget billions of dollars in the red, most planning goals have been put on hold. Californians, like many Americans these days, continue to fight any new taxes, even for fire protection in the wake of devastating conflagrations. Eventually, something (or someone) will have to give.

For most of the 1990s, the city of San Diego did not even have a planning department. The department was eliminated in the early 1990s and much of the remaining staff were moved to more politically correct areas such as economic development. After the mayoral elections of 2000, the planning department was reinstated just in time for California's severe budget crisis.

The problem in southern California is that many people have opted for the privatization of urban services. The vast majority of new residential projects are planned unit developments complete with a wide variety or covenants and restrictions. Many of them are gated and thus completely removed form the public realm. Within these communities, "shadow governments" make all of the decisions internally with little regard for what is happening in nearby areas. Much of the region is thus carved up into competing city-states. Meaningful comprehensive planning is thus difficult.

This brings us back to the question of who gets the blame or the credit for what has gone on in the region. Given the difficulty of deciding whether San Diego is well planned or poorly planned, I have opted to concentrate on the ways individual people and communities have sought to create and sustain meaningful neighborhoods. The issues are not entirely independent, of course, but the emphasis in this book is less about top-down governmental decision making than it is about historical accident, whimsy, and the search for a sense of place.

NOTES

Chapter 1. San Diego Images: Inventing a Mediterranean Paradise

1. Ernst Griffin, "Peopling the Region," in *San Diego: An Introduction to the Region*, ed. Phillip Pryde (Dubuque, Iowa: Kendall Hunt, 1992), 69–83.

2. See, for example, Raymond Starr, *San Diego: A Pictorial History* (Norfolk, Va.: Donning, 1986) and Richard F. Pourade, *The Silver Dons* (San Diego: Union-Tribune, 1963).

3. Richard Henry Dana, *Two Years Before the Mast* (New York: Harper, 1840).

4. Dana, as quoted in Imre Quastler, "San Diegans on the Move," in Pryde, *San Diego: An Introduction*, 167.

5. Elizabeth Macphail, *The Story of New Town San Diego and Its Founder, Alonzo E. Horton* (San Diego: San Diego Historical Society, 1979).

6. Starr, *San Diego: A Pictorial History*, 118.

7. Helen Hunt Jackson, *Ramona: A Story* (Boston: Roberts Brothers, 1882).

8. See, for example, Old San Diego Review Board, *Old San Diego Architectural and Site Development Standards and Criteria* (San Diego: City of San Diego, 1972) and Linda Zombeck, "A Study of Land Use Patterns in Old Town San Diego," Master's thesis, San Diego State University, 1986.

9. See, for example, Thomas Joseph Adema, *Our Hills and Valleys: A History of the Helix-Spring Valley Region* (San Diego: San Diego Historical Society, 1993) and Phillip Pryde, "The Most Essential Resource," in Pryde, *San Diego: An Introduction*, 118–38.

10. Florence Christman, *The Romance of Balboa Park* (San Diego: San Diego Historical Society, 1985).

11. Christopher Lukinbeal, "'On Location' in San Diego: Film, Television, and Urban Thirdspace," Ph.D. dissertation, San Diego State University, 2000.

12. Bob O'Brien, "Fun in the Sun: Regional Recreation Facilities," in Pryde, *San Diego: An Introduction*, 243–57.

13. David McArthur, "Building the Region: The Geomorphology of San Diego County," in Pryde, *San Diego: An Introduction*, 13–30.

14. See, for example, Richard F. Pourade, *The Rising Tide* (San Diego: Union-Tribune Publishing Company, 1966).

15. Daniel Arreola and James Curtis, *The Mexican Border Cities: Landscape Anatomy and Place Personality* (Tucson: University of Arizona Press, 1993).

16. Starr, *San Diego: A Pictorial History*, 203.

17. San Diego Regional Economic Development Corporation (hereafter SDREDC), *San Diego Book of Facts: Local Economy*, 2001, www.signonsandiego.com/bookoffacts/.

18. James Blick, "Working the Land: Agriculture in San Diego County," in Pryde, *San Diego: An Introduction*, 139–54.

19. Kevin Lynch, *The Image of the City* (Cambridge, Mass.: MIT Press, 1960).

Chapter 2. San Diego Realities: Social and Economic Trends

1. All population figures are from the U.S. Census, Department of Commerce, Bureau of the Census, 1880 through 2000.

2. Carl Abbott, *Greater Portland: Urban Life and Landscape in the Pacific Northwest* (Philadelphia: University of Pennsylvania Press, 2001).

3. Demographia.com, 2000 Census: U.S. Municipalities over 50,000 Ranked by 2000 Population.

4. "Top Ten Cities for Hispanics," *Hispanic Magazine*, July–August 2002.

5. "Best Places for Business," *Forbes Magazine*, May 27, 2002, 128.

6. Forbes.com, Best Places for Business and Careers, 2003.

7. San Diego Regional Economic Development Corporation (SDREDC), *San Diego Book of Facts: Local Economy*, 2001, www.signonsandiego.com/bookoffacts/.

8. San Diego County, Department of Agriculture, *Agricultural Crops and Natural Resources* (annual), 2001.

9. SDREDC, *San Diego Book of Facts: Business and Employment*, 2001, 12.

10. SDREDC, *San Diego Book of Facts: Tourism*, 2001, 2–3.

11. San Diego Association of Governments (SANDAG), *Indicators of Sustainable Competitiveness: San Diego Region*, 2002, 40–42, 60–64.

12. SANDAG, *Indicators of Sustainable Competitiveness*, 13.

13. David Reiff, *Los Angeles: Capital of the Third World* (New York: Simon and Schuster, 1991).

14. Lawrence A. Herzog, *Where North Meets South: Cities, Space, and Politics on the U.S.-Mexico Border* (Austin: Center for Mexican-American Studies, University of Texas, 1990).

15. Phillip Pryde, "The Most Essential Resource," in *San Diego: An Introduction to the Region*, ed. Phillip Pryde (Dubuque, Iowa: Kendall Hunt, 1992), 120.

16. Thomas Oberhauser, *Rare Plants and Habitats in San Diego County* (San Diego: County Department of Planning and Land Use, 1990).

17. Kevin Lynch and Donald Appleyard, *Temporary Paradise: A Look at the Special Landscape of the San Diego Region* (San Diego: Marston Family, 1974).

18. SANDAG, *Indicators of Sustainable Competitiveness*.

Chapter 3. Lifestyle Zones in the Central City

1. See, for example, Truman Hartshorn, 1992. *Interpreting the City: An Urban Geography.* (New York: Wiley, 1992), 231–34.

2. Michael Dear and Steven Flusty, "Postmodern Urbanism," *Annals of the Association of American Geographers* 88, 1 (1998): 50–72.

3. Reyner Banham, *Los Angeles: The Architecture of Four Ecologies* (New York: Harper and Row, 1971).

4. Walter Firey, *Land Use in Central Boston* (Cambridge, Mass.: Harvard University Press, 1947).

5. Kevin Lynch, *The Image of the City* (Cambridge, Mass.: MIT Press. 1960).

6. Kevin Lynch, *Managing the Sense of Region* (Cambridge, Mass.: MIT Press, 1976).

7. See, for example, Yi-Fu Tuan, *Space and Place: The Perspective of Experience* (Minneapolis: University of Minnesota Press, 1977) and Edward C. Relph, *Place and Placelessness* (London: Pion, 1976).

8. Brenda Kayzar, "First Let Me Tell You About the Neighborhood: The Residential

Sorting Process and Place Identity Promotion," Master's thesis, San Diego State University, 2001.

9. Michael J. Weiss, *The Clustering of America* (New York: Harper and Row, 1988).

10. Ruth Varney Held, *Beach Town: Early Days in Ocean Beach* (San Diego: Held, 1975).

11. James Christopher Carter, "Ocean Beach: Continuity and Change in a San Diego Community," Master's thesis, San Diego State University, 1993.

12. Larry Ford and Ernst Griffin, 1979, "Ghettoization in Paradise," *Geographical Review* 69 (1979): 140–58.

13. Daniel Arreola, "Mexican American Housescapes," *Geographical Review* 78 (1988): 229–315.

14. Robert Rundle, "Historic Preservation and Adaptive Landscape Modification in Golden Hill, Sherman Heights, and Grant Hill, San Diego," Master's thesis, San Diego State University, 1998.

15. Larry Ford and Ernst Griffin, "Chicano Park: Personalizing an Institutional Landscape," *Landscape* 25 (1981): 42–46.

16. Thomas H. Baumann, *Kensington-Talmadge: 1910–1997* (San Diego: Kensington-Talmadge Community Association, 1997).

17. Centre City Development Corporation website, www.ccdc.com/

18. Larry Ford, *America's New Downtowns: Revitalization or Reinvention?* (Baltimore: Johns Hopkins University Press, 2003).

19. Jacques Gordon, *Horton Plaza: A Case Study of Private Development* (Cambridge, Mass.: MIT Center for Real Estate Development, 1985).

20. Ford, *America's New Downtowns*.

21. Phillip Pryde, "The Most Essential Resource," in *San Diego: An Introduction to the Region*, ed. Phillip Pryde (Dubuque, Iowa: Kendall Hunt, 1992), 133–38.

22. Michael Neal, "Mission Valley Community Plan: Looking Forward," Master's thesis, San Diego State University, 1996.

23. Joel Garreau, *Edge City: Life on the New Frontier* (New York: Doubleday, 1991).

Chapter 4. Lifestyle Zones on the Edge of Town

1. Patricia Schaelchlin, *La Jolla: The Story of a Community, 1887–1987* (San Diego: Friends of the La Jolla Library, 1988), 33.

2. Lawrence Herzog, *Where North Meets South: Cities, Space, and Politics on the U.S.-Mexico Border* (Austin: Center for Mexican American Studies, University of Texas, 1990), 107.

3. Herzog, *Where North Meets South*, 155.

4. Ernst Griffin and Larry Ford, "A Model of Latin American City Structure," *Geographical Review* 70 (1980): 397–422.

5. Thomas Joseph Adema, *Our Hills and Valleys: A History of the Helix-Spring Valley Region* (San Diego: San Diego Historical Society, 1993).

6. D. W. Meinig, ed., *The Interpretation of Ordinary Landscapes: Geographical Essays* (New York: Oxford University Press, 1979).

7. Brenda Kayzar, "First Let Me Tell You About the Neighborhood: The Residential Sorting Process and Place Identity Promotion," Master's thesis, San Diego State University, 2001.

8. Phillip Langdon, *A Better Place to Live: Reshaping the American Suburb* (Amherst: University of Massachusetts Press, 1994)

9. SANDAG, "San Diego Region Population Growth," in *A Map for All Seasons* (Calendar) (San Diego: San Diego Association of Governments, 1999/2000).

10. Hans P. Johnson, Juan Onésimo Sandoval, and Sonya M. Tafoya, *Who's Your Neighbor? Residential Segregation and Diversity in California*, California Counts: Population Trends and Profiles 4, no. 1 (San Francisco: Public Policy Institute of California, 2002).

11. Christopher Lukinbeal, "'On Location' in San Diego: Film, Television, and Urban Thirdspace," Ph.D. dissertation, San Diego State University, 2000.

12. Roger Barnett, "The Libertarian Suburb: Deliberate Disorder," *Landscape* 22 (1978): 44–48.

13. Lakeside Historical Society, *Legends of Lakeside* (Lakeside, Calif.: Lakeside Historical Society, 1985).

Chapter 5. Communities Beyond the Fringe

1. Clifford Trafzer and Richard Carrico, 1992, "American Indians: The County's First Residents," in *San Diego: An Introduction to the Region*, ed. Phillip Pryde (Dubuque, Iowa: Kendall Hunt, 1992), 51–68.

2. David Murray, *Indian Giving: Economies of Power in Indian-White Exchanges* (Amherst: University of Massachusetts Press, 2000).

3. Cheryl Hinton, *Barona Spirits Speak*, Barona Cultural Center and Museum, 2003.

4. Julian websites, www.desertusa.com.cities/ca/julian.html and www.julianca .com/history/index.htm.

5. Anza-Borrego Desert State Park websites, www.desertusa.com/anza-borrego/ du-abp-map.html and www.borregovalleyinn.com/history.htm.

6. SANDAG, "San Diego Region Population Growth," in *A Map for All Seasons* (Calendar) (San Diego: San Diego Association of Governments, 1999/2000).

7. Brenda Kayzar, "First Let me Tell You About the Neighborhood: The Residential Sorting Process and Place Identity Promotion," Master's thesis, San Diego State University, 2001.

8. Fallbrook website, www.fallbrookca.org/nearby.htm.

9. Temecula Valley Wine Country website, www.temeculawines.org/map.asp.

10. Langdon Sully and Taryn Bigelow, *Oceanside: Crest of the Wave* (Northridge, Calif.: Windsor Publications, 1988).

11. Camp Pendleton website, Base Facts and Stats, www.pe.net/~rksnow/ cacounty/camppendleton.htm#statistics

12. Kevin Lynch, *The Image of the City* (Cambridge, Mass.: MIT Press, 1960).

Epilogue: Planning in "America's Finest City"

1. Richard Hogan, *The Failure of Planning: Permitting Sprawl in San Diego Suburbs, 1970–1999* (Columbus: Ohio State University Press, 2003) and Gene Bunnell, *Making Places Special: Stories of Real Places Made Better Through Planning* (Chicago: Planners Press, 2002).

INDEX